When Men Grieve

When Men Grieve

*Why Men Grieve Differently
and How You Can Help*

Elizabeth Levang, Ph.D.

Fairview Press
Minneapolis, Minnesota

Published by Fairview Press, 2450 Riverside Avenue South, Minneapolis, MN 55454.

Library of Congress Cataloging-in-Publication Data
    When men grieve : why men grieve differently and how you can help / Elizabeth Levang.
            p.   cm.
    Includes bibliographical references.
    ISBN 1-57749-078-9 (paperback : alk. paper)
    1. Men—Psychology.   2. Grief.   3. Grief—Case studies.
4. Loss (Psychology).   5. Loss (Psychology)—Case studies.   I. Title.
    BF692.5.L48   1998
    155.9'37'081—dc21   98-28694
                                                                 CIP

First Printing: October 1998

Printed in the United States of America
03 02 01 00   7 6 5 4 3 2

Cover design: Laurie Duren
Text design: Dorie McClelland

Acknowledgments for previously published work: "Follow the Wind, Songs for Stained Souls" by Ralph Robinson contains song lyrics from the compact disc of the same name; reprinted by permission of Ralph Robinson. Portions of "Follow the Wind, Songs for Stained Souls" by Ralph Robinson first appeared as "Follow the Wind … Creation of a Dream" in *We Need Not Walk Alone* (1998); reprinted by permission of Ralph Robinson and The Compassionate Friends.

For a free current catalog of Fairview Press titles, call toll-free 1-800-544-8207.

To my grandmother, Salute Del Bel Belluz,
whose love for me made all the difference.

Contents

Contents

Acknowledgments

A slight breeze tickled our faces as the three of us—Rachel Faldet, Karen Fitton, and I—sat on the train platform in Norwalk, Connecticut. It was early July, and moments earlier we had tried to cajole our cabdriver into speeding just a little faster so we would catch the next train into Manhattan. We had finished taping another television program and were at the end of our book tour promoting Rachel and Karen's *Our Stories of Miscarriage*. By the time we handed the cabdriver his fare, the train had already pulled away from the station. As we settled back to wait for the next train, it seemed appropriate to talk about where our lives were headed. Karen and Rachel encouraged me that day to pursue my longtime interest in writing a book on men and grief. I thank them both for that important nudge. I especially want to thank Rachel, whose role with this project seemed to mushroom with time. It has meant a great deal to be able to count on her literary expertise and her friendship.

My husband, Curt, not only read every word I wrote, but contributed in many other ways as well. His skills as a clinical psychologist are imprinted throughout the book, and I thank him for his expert advice. Over the many months I researched and wrote this book, my daughter, Natalie, was always quick to share her wisdom and love. I thank her for the many sacrifices she made and for her unfailing support.

The evocative poetry found within this book was composed expressly for each chapter by Louis Cerulli, a truly magnificent poet. Louis also took on the demanding task of helping me locate contributors and was responsible for editing their stories. I thank Louis for sharing his creative gifts and for his patience during this ever-evolving project.

I am in awe of the men who contributed their stories to this book. It takes great courage to share the intimate pain of grief, and I have felt humbled and privileged to know these men through their writing. I thank them for letting me, and you, into their lives.

Many hands and voices lent support to my work. For all those who hammered out ideas with me, prayed, shared personal experiences, listened, read drafts, and kept my project in their heart, I offer my sincere thanks. Among these dear hearts I would like to thank Jill Cerulli, Brenda Crowe, and Kay Talbot, Ph.D. I especially want to thank my sister, Julie Ehrman, and husband, Terry, for their constant support and for their special care and concern for my family; Karol Dahlof, who helped me with the research, arranging sessions and taking copious notes; Ken Druck, Ph.D., who spent many hours sharing his clinical expertise on the subject of men and also that of his own painful journey surviving the death of his daughter, Jenna; and to Richard Edler, whose efforts at transforming his life after the death of his son, Mark, have been an inspiration to me. I am most grateful to the men and women who graciously allowed me to interview them and learn from their suffering, and to the friends and colleagues who helped me network around the country in search of subjects and contributors.

I offer special thanks to Lane Stiles at Fairview Press, whose belief in my ideas and abilities gave me strength.

Introduction

I am Italian. Full-blooded. This heritage likely conjures up images of a family that is not afraid to show emotions. In part this was true in my family; I knew when my parents were angry or disappointed. It was not too difficult to know when they were pleased, either. But sadness or grief was another story altogether. I do not believe I have ever seen my father cry. I think I never will. Tears are not a part of his manly world.

When I was working on my first book, *Remembering with Love: Messages of Hope for the First Year of Grieving and Beyond,* I was bewildered by the resistance that men exhibited to talking about their feelings. I thought that was just how my father and other male relatives acted. I asked dozens of men I knew to write a few lines or even a short paragraph about the death of a loved one so that I could include their thoughts and experiences in the book. While many men endorsed the project and were quite excited about the book, few were willing to share their feelings. Those few who did, spoke of powerful emotions and intense pain. It seemed that these men were uncomfortable, yet they were willing to put aside their apprehension so that they might help others. It was all very puzzling to me.

My husband, Curt, was one of those men who were reluctant to talk.

I have seen Curt cry. It has happened just a handful of times in the sixteen years we have been married. His tears always come as a shock to me. Yet I am trying very hard to understand what his tears mean and how I should respond to them. I know that even though it's difficult for him to live out the stereotypically tough, masculine role, being vulnerable is difficult, too. My husband is a clinical psychologist. He knows what emotions are; he can usually name his feelings. But, like many women, I sometimes fail to recognize them.

The first time my husband cried was in response to our ongoing struggle with infertility. For four years we had gone the route of endless exams and tests, exploratory surgery, and more testing. The diagnosis never changed: unexplainable infertility. We investigated our options for adoption—a three-year waiting list, if we were lucky enough to qualify. We thought about a childless lifestyle. Month after agonizing month, we followed all the procedures—and waited.

One night in June Curt sat on the edge of our bed and blurted out in a quivering voice, "I don't want another Father's Day to go by without being a father." I had forgotten that Father's Day was coming in just a few days. As he uttered these words, his eyes filled with tears, and he began to sob uncontrollably. Fours years of testing, four years of bad news, four years of missed Father's Days. He could not control the turmoil any longer. I felt helpless and ignorant. How had I overlooked his pain?

The next Father's Day came and went, and so did the next. Not until three years later did Curt's dream come true, and then only because of two skillful physicians, a perceptive nurse, and the grace of God. That was the second time that Curt cried.

The last words from our fertility specialist had been, "You'll never have a child. Certainly not without medical intervention." Our only hope was in vitro fertilization, but the success rate was so poor and the costs so high we had opted to let nature take its course. I had been feeling rather ill for more than a month, and Curt casually remarked that I might be pregnant. Though neither of us dared believe it, he bought a home pregnancy test anyway. To our utter amazement the test turned up positive. A second test at the clinic again showed positive.

"What do I do next?" I complacently asked the clinic representative who had called to confirm the testing. We were still afraid to get excited.

In disbelief, we headed for an ultrasound. Our fertility specialist was not reassuring, but when he saw the heartbeat on the monitor, he was at a complete loss for words. As we sat in his office, he paged quickly through my file—all five inches of it—and kept mumbling about inconclusive tests. Yes, I was pregnant.

My water broke on the coldest day of the year. Christmas was only a few days away, and recent ice storms had made travel difficult. My sister Julie, worried about our safety and the treacherous drive, demanded that I get to the hospital and stay there, even if we had to wait in the coffee shop all night.

When I arrived at the hospital late that afternoon, they wheeled me into a delivery room. There we waited out the night. My back hurt so bad that I finally was given a spinal block. In the morning my obstetrician, Dr. Hachiya, came into the room, and within minutes we were well on our way to delivering our long-awaited child. Or so we thought. The baby didn't come, her heartbeat dropped, and the room suddenly swarmed with staff. The floor supervisor, an ex-army nurse, stood on a stool over my abdomen, pushing down on me with all her might and barking into my ear, "If you want this baby to live, you'd better start pushing now." The umbilical cord was tightly wrapped around the baby's neck.

A few tense minutes later, Dr. Hachiya was able to free our baby from the cord and lay her on my stomach. She was not breathing. Her face was gray-blue. She sputtered and choked on the fluids in her throat and could not cry. I tried talking, calling to Curt to look at her. The nurse reached above my head, put an oxygen mask over the baby's face, and within seconds took her to the Neonatal Intensive Care Unit (NICU).

Dr. Wiborg-Harvath, a pediatrician doing rounds that morning, happened to step on the ward just as our Natalie was being brought in. She took one look at her and raced to get the baby stabilized. Later that day, after the delivery nurse, Audrey Gable, had misgivings about the placenta, Natalie was thought to have also contracted Group B strep, an infection that kills babies because of their deficient immune systems. In addition to the oxygen and antibiotics being given to her to clear the pocket of air that had collected around her heart, a second course of antibiotics was introduced. We waited for hopeful news.

Curt busied himself by fielding calls from worried friends and conferring with the hospital staff. He wiped my tears and worked very hard to buoy my sagging optimism. He held Natalie with sweet tenderness and would negotiate for just a few minutes longer when a nurse would come to return her to the NICU. I have no idea when he slept or ate.

Christmas passed. Natalie's unopened presents stood vigil under the tree.

Dr. Hachiya discharged me from the hospital, but I returned early each morning to spend every possible moment in the NICU cradling Natalie, talking to her, being afraid for her. Curt and I, and some of my family, spent evenings holding her and staring into her innocent face. In as clear and unwavering a voice as he could muster, Curt read poems by Robert Frost to Natalie. Reluctantly, Curt decided to go back to work and tend to his clients.

One afternoon I was left standing by the nurses' station. Natalie's IV tube had collapsed, and a nurse was inserting a new line—delicate work on such small veins. I was tired, frightened. I turned and saw Curt approaching me. Surprised, I wondered if something had gone wrong. I called to him, "What are you doing here?" He came up close and hung his head. "I decided I needed help more than my clients," he said slowly. The significance of his words left me breathless. Tears rolled down his cheeks. He had tried to be brave for me, for Natalie, but he was afraid, too. He felt his dream of being a father slipping away. His masculinity, his identity, was in jeopardy. Once again, I had not seen his pain. I had counted on his support, which he had given, but I was oblivious to his fears and the terrible strain he had been living under.

The grief that Curt experienced about fatherhood has made him a more attentive and sensitive father. He has worked to be more forthright with his feelings, even when he thinks I will not be able to understand them. For my part, I try to listen more carefully to Curt's silences and to empathize with the pressure he feels to be strong. Our dear Natalie has gained a unique perspective on men and grief, for we have shared the story of her birth and talked openly about our pain. At seven years old, she still delights in telling anyone who will listen that she made her daddy's dreams come true.

My interest in men and grief is part of my life story. If you are reading this, grief is likely a part of your story, too. I trust that you will find this book helpful in understanding your partner's grief, and your own. I trust, too, that you will walk away feeling encouraged and hopeful. This book was written expressly for these reasons.

The essays of eleven men—fathers, spouses, brothers,

friends—are found within the pages of this book. It took courage for these men to write about their personal tragedies, and that is why the stories are so special, so important to me. I hope they will become special and important to you, too. It took Curt and me many years to understand that we grieve differently. We are still learning. The lessons we can gain from men like John Jankord, Larry Johnson, Kent Koppelman, and Ralph Robinson are powerful. Their message is that men do grieve. They do care. They may grieve differently, but they grieve equally.

At the end of every chapter, you will find a specific response to consider. I invite you to think about these helping responses and to let them inspire you. These are meant to challenge your beliefs about men and grief, while also equipping you with new strategies to help men grieve. These responses are also intended to validate your feelings, desires, and hopes.

This book necessarily rests on generalizations drawn from the lives and situations of many men and women. As it is impossible for me to know the unique circumstances of your life, some statements or thoughts may not apply to you, and others may ring true. As with all books, take what fits, what resonates in your own heart. This is not a book about what is "right" or "wrong" about grieving men, about intimate relationships, or about women. It is a book about understanding what is and what can be.

Thank you for letting our lives cross. I wish you peace.

—Elizabeth Levang

PART ONE

NEW UNDERSTANDINGS

1

When Men and Women Grieve

My grief trembles in tree limbs,
Quiet on Winter's fingers.
Like frozen lightening
Blackened on dusk's canvas,
It struggles in the crippled air.
Every evening I walk with it,
Tangled on each foggy breath,
An ever-tightening knot.

—Louis Cerulli

Follow the Wind, Songs for Stained Souls

The ambulance came out of the subdivision, but the lights were not flashing, the sirens were not blaring, and the driver was not in a hurry. I should have put it together. It was not until my wife, Kathy, and I drove up to our house and I saw the yellow police tape that I realized something was wrong.

Running to the house, I ducked under the yellow tape. "Who are you?" asked three deputy sheriffs as they surrounded me. "I'm Ryan's father. How is he?" The deputy immediately in front of me looked me in the eyes and said, "I'm sorry, sir. He's gone." I felt trapped, claustrophobic. I could not breathe. My knees buckled, and I collapsed.

As Ryan's friends were running around the yard screaming and crying, I managed to walk numbly to the car to tell Kathy that our sixteen-year-old son was dead.

A gathering of teenagers, alcohol, and a handgun the kids had found changed my life. Ryan and his friends had removed the clip from the gun "just to be safe." They had all played with the gun. They fired it into the air, into the fireplace. They pointed it at each other. When Ryan played with the gun, the safety, somehow, was turned off. The one live bullet in the chamber ended his life. The coroner told me that death was instantaneous. He doubted that Ryan even heard the gun go off.

Ryan's years were full, albeit short. My son's accomplishments on stage as a young actor were impressive. An athlete, Ryan gave up sports as his passion for acting, music, writing, and poetry matured. He was self-confident. I recognized his fearlessness, and I respected it. Fearlessness had been a part of Ryan from an early age.

My grief wore many faces; each could arouse a torrent of thought and emotion. Grief was disguised in Ryan's favorite foods we no longer bought, his clothes that no longer needed washing, and his guitar that no one played. It could be a reflection off the lake that once carried our canoe or the words to a song he loved. It lurked in my dreams. The wind sounded like Ryan crying.

In the beginning, I would collapse and cry. I felt like a rodent in an emotional maze from which I could not escape. I could not climb out, there was no exit, and I always ended up back where I had started. At times reminders of Ryan came like waves on the beach. The ones I could see coming I stepped over, or I allowed them to pass through me. Other reminders came from behind, with no warning, and knocked me to the ground.

On the first anniversary of my son's death, I walked to the cemetery, listening on headphones to the songs that had been played at Ryan's school memorial service. A delivery truck came over the crest of the hill, and I had an eerie intuition that I needed to stop the truck. I was not expecting anything, but I waved the driver down and asked if she had something for the Robinsons. She looked at me with surprise. I signed for the package, tucked it under my arm, and continued walking.

As I walked through the cemetery, I saw what looked like a white ribbon on the ground trailing away from the far side of Ryan's headstone. Ryan's friends had left an assortment of items there over the year: fishing lures, compact discs, notes, pinwheels, flowers, key chains, poems. Why a white ribbon? I wondered. When the headstone was in full view, I realized the ribbon was the strap to an electric guitar. Remembering Ryan's love of guitar, I fell to my knees and sobbed. I felt like clawing at the earth to get my son out from where he lay.

Later, after talking to Ryan, I opened the package. Inside were two gift-wrapped boxes and a handwritten message from a close friend. At the top of the note my friend had written, "In Memory of

Ryan Jon Robinson." *My friend said he had purchased an assortment of compact discs a year ago, on the weekend Ryan had died.
Ironically, all the discs included songs about the death of a loved
one. As a tribute to Ryan, my friend sent me these songs on an
audio tape and included a cherry wood box to store the tape in.*

*I played the tape. After the first song, though, I thought I
would never be able to listen to it entirely. The words brought up
too much pain. Richard Shindell sang, "There was never any warning / There was never any sign / It's just that I woke up this morning / And eternity was mine." I knew this sentiment too well; I did-
n't need music to remind me of it. Weren't Ryan's death, my memories, and my nightmares enough? Shindell's song continued, "But
you don't know what you're dealing with, you haven't got a clue."
How I wish I didn't know what I was dealing with, I thought.*

*Several days later, on the way to work, I listened to the tape
again. As I drove, the lyrics from a Catie Curtis song mocked me,
"It just gets harder when you ask why." How many times had I
asked that question? I wondered. Why him? Why us? Why our
family? Why a sixteen-year-old boy with talent, with so much to
give? The Curtis song continued, "I'm tired from all the weight /
I'm tired of being strong." I remembered the times since Ryan's
death I had thought about ending my own life. Being alive hurt
too much. It was a matter of balance. I thought being alive with
my pain had to be worse than my own death. I was tired of being
strong.*

*Still driving, I listened to Diane Zeigler's song. She sang, "I
fell to my knees at my brother's grave / Seven full years since he
passed away." The words made me cry. I remembered collapsing
at Ryan's grave when I saw the guitar. As I continued along the
freeway, people stared at me from their car windows. I didn't
care what people thought. I let myself go with my tears, and it*

felt good.

I found that the drive to work in the morning was the best time for me to listen to the tape. I welcomed the solitude, the privacy provided by the insulated chamber of my car. I was working my way through all of these songs, one by one. Each held a meaning, each unleashed emotions that I was better off not tucking away. I started to let go of pent-up frustration, rage, and sadness. I would arrive at work after my forty-minute commute with blurry, bloodshot eyes. I started carrying tissues in the car.

An Archie Roach song made me realize that it is impossible to understand how much a parent loves a child until that child is gone. Words from a Steve Fisher song helped me realize that much of my life had been defined by Ryan's life. Most children, I thought, can't understand how much of their parents' lives are explained by their daily activities. I thought of my two living daughters.

Eventually, my wife, Kathy, and I attended a regional meeting of a bereavement organization for parents and siblings. Over three hundred people were there, all listening to the main speaker. It was a bittersweet feeling as I realized I wasn't the only one who had experienced a terrible loss.

Later that day, we broke into smaller groups. Kathy and I sat with people dealing with "tragic loss"—death with no anticipation or warning. Amazed at the stories of death, I listened attentively. Though it seemed impossible, there were losses that seemed more tragic than ours: children from the same family who died at the same time, children who battled with crippling diseases, children who had been murdered.

As I listened to these stories, the words from a Dougie MacLean song on the tape came to mind. In my head, he sang, "These broken wings won't fly / These broken wings won't fly...at all." In fact, all day long at the meeting I heard songs in my head.

Besides connecting with the grief organization, I also had been seeing a therapist who told me "to keep the grief moving, don't deny it or suppress it." At some point, I turned the corner. I could listen to the songs on the tape without inconsolable sobbing. I could think of Ryan and smile.

The songs had helped me. I decided that they should be available to anyone—not just me—dealing with the death of a loved one. I realized that music can help people deal with grief in a productive manner. I felt I had a mission.

Over time, I contacted each of the musicians and put together a compact disc. The title, Follow the Wind: Songs for Stained Souls, *was inspired by one of Ryan's poems I found after his death. Ryan had written, "Follow the wind to other sides that call to you. Can you capture the life that has yet to be lived? That stained soul can be cleaned with time and faith."*

After I finished making the compact disc, I reached a level of acceptance of Ryan's death that I never thought possible. For me, the music and my involvement with the bereavement organization were important parts of coping with grief.

My son is in my heart every day.

In my heart are also Richard Shindell's lyrics, "But you are half a world away. There is little now that I can say but that I'll always love you and I'll always miss you and you are always welcome here."

—Ralph O. Robinson

Grief is an inescapable experience. There is little way to hide from the emotional suffering the death of someone we love causes, and no possibility of insulating ourselves from a world that includes job loss, catastrophic illness, divorce, abuse, harassment, and rape. Grief creates intense anguish and undeniable pain. It is complex and continuous. No matter how hard we try to outrun it, the possibility of grief is ever present in our lives.

While grief is inevitable, most people are unprepared for the tumultuous feelings and thoughts it brings. The trauma of death or loss leaves many of us feeling anxious, numb, isolated, shocked, confused, empty, depressed, irritable, angry, sad. Grief feels hostile and foreign, and we are uncertain how to go on. A sense of being paralyzed and immobilized by cold reality takes root.

Grief creates a sense of chaos. It destroys our connection with a familiar, patterned, and comfortable reality. It robs us of our dreams and cheats us out of our future. What was, has ended. While the world continues on, bustling and vibrant, our world has stopped. Time stands still for us. Despite our feelings, tomorrow continues to come.

Grief irrevocably changes our life. What we believed yesterday may no longer hold any truth. Our mind reels from the pain of opportunities squandered, of unkind or harsh words spoken, and of promises made that were never kept. Whatever we think life may have prepared us for, we are always naive about grief. Grieving is a test of real courage and the tenacity of the human spirit. Grief ever reminds us of the fragility of life and of the need to live life in the moment. The previous story by Ralph Robinson tells of these solemn truths.

The depth of pain and anguish that death or loss brings convinces us that we are helpless and incapable of surviving. We want a magical answer, or at the very least we want a way to gauge the time it will take to heal—some guarantee that we will not suffer for eternity. The act of grieving is debilitating and exhausting. Its duration is indefinite.

Grief causes trauma to our physical, emotional, spiritual, and cognitive selves. Our chest and abdomen ache endlessly. We have trouble breathing, concentrating, and thinking. We experience social isolation and economic pressures. Friends, family, and co-workers may be sources of consolation and encouragement, or they may be uncaring and lacking in understanding. We may hear our fill of empty platitudes and mindless cliches, or we may be fortunate enough to discover a support network to reassure and assist us. Our religious faith may be tested as we wrestle with the thought of how something bad could happen to us. For far too many, death may seem like the only relief from the oppressive weight of grieving.

When we try to ignore or deny grief, it finds ways of making itself known. Grief does not evaporate or dissipate because we ignore our emotions. Those emotions just express themselves in other, indirect, avenues. Addiction, abuse, or other destructive behaviors make poor substitutes for the work of grieving. For many, avoidance leads to despair and depression—an inability to find even a glimmer of hope on the sunniest day. Grief is not a gracious host. It takes its leave when it's ready, not when we're ready.

No two people experience grief in exactly the same manner. Whether male or female, old or young, Swedish or Native American, Protestant or Roman Catholic, grief is an individual process. It is as unique as the rhythmic beating of one's heart or the kaleidoscopic landscape of one's mind. Our grief is ours alone. How we react, process, or survive grief depends on a host of factors that only we are privy to. There are no easy five-step recipes, no templates that determine, manage, or pre-scribe how each of us will grieve. After all, we are individuals.

Though expressed in unique and individual ways, grief does tend to manifest itself in broad patterns and processes. Many people say they have found some comfort in knowing what stages or steps of grief they might experience as they struggle to heal. Yet a map does not exist that can precisely define our way through grief. What we have are mere guidelines, rays of light that illuminate our darkened and narrow path. As many people come to know, the process of grieving is not easily defined.

Life is about change and the occasions change presents for growth, adaptation, renewal. Sometimes we tolerate or permit change. At other times we are swept passively into it, unable to resist its forceful power. Grief is the steward of change. The many choices and decisions we face in our grief will undeniably alter our life path. Our world has changed, externally and internally. There is no going back, no way to recapture the past. We are in a wretched state of uncertainty.

Many of us respond to grief with denial, rage, bitterness, and despair. We rail against the devastation that has occurred and fight desperately to control what is left of our life. Others come to treat grief as a discovery process and allow it to trans-form their attitudes, priorities, and perspective on life. They persist in overcoming their life crisis and cling to the promise of healing. So much good in our world, like Ralph's efforts to bring music into our grieving, can be attributed to those who address causes and concerns that grow out of their pain.

Change is inevitable in grief, but it is rarely predictable. Healing does happen, life does develop a new rhythm and pat-tern, but how or when this will occur is part of the vast unknown of grieving. Grief cannot be rushed or hurried along.

Grief is an experience like no other in life. Most of us find it impossible to comprehend the harsh turn our life has taken, and we search frenziedly for order, sanity, and compassion. What people desire, almost instantaneously, and sometimes secretly, is support. We know we cannot face our tragedy alone, and we cannot survive in solitude. Grief is a time of need.

Yet tragedy often separates people and makes more obvious the radical differences in coping styles. This division is most apparent between genders. At a time when grieving parents want to cling to each other to make sense of a child's cruel and untimely death, when out-of-work husbands want their wife's encouragement while searching for new employment, when a cancer-stricken woman wants her mate's understanding as she faces a grueling course of radiation and surgery, the sexes are often unable to communicate their grief or enlist each other's support.

Men and women who are intimate partners have a privileged connection forged by love, respect, and admiration. This connection gives couples an enormous capacity for comforting and providing solace to each other. In its best sense, the bond gives couples the ability to look beyond differences and to firmly grasp the lifeline of hope. "Different" does not have to mean bad or wrong, inferior or deficient. And "different" does not have to result in an absence of communication and support.

We all want to grieve well. Yet too often men and women deny their partner's pain and attempt to legislate how they are to grieve. Women tend to perceive men as being void of emotion and loath to verbalize their anguish. To women, men seem to have no feelings, no words. They appear to have no language for grief, no ability to hang words on their experience. Women are often bewildered when the occasional tear drops silently during a movie or when a quick sob intrudes on some distant background music. They wonder if that one expression of sorrow is the sum extent of his grief.

Many women talk about their feelings with seemingly little effort. They appear willing to share openly their cries, tears, and sobs. Grief is rarely inhibited; rather, many women tend to express it outwardly and publicly. The woman's actions seem to stand in stark contrast to the man's apparent stoicism and lack of feeling, which the woman perceives as evidence that the man simply does not care. Women conclude that men are as cold and hardened as the inky black bars of a prison cell. Justified or not, they declare men unfeeling and incapable of true love.

Men tend to feel just as baffled by women's ways of grieving. Many men grow weary of tears and crying, and admonish their partner for what they regard as self-inflicted pain. Apparently disinclined to indulge themselves in a similar fashion, these men distract themselves from their grief in order to go on with the business of living. Lest grief control them, they work to steel themselves against their fragile emotions and to keep their pain private. These men question why their partner ruminates and insists on telling and retelling their tragedy. Men know the story is forever etched on the walls of their mind; they have no need to be reminded. Eventually, many men become angry or disillusioned when they sense they have failed to repair the gaping hole in their partner's heart.

The sexes have very different languages for grief. The ways they process their emotions are unique, too. Men tend to *think* their way through grief; their intellect is their guide. Women seem to *feel* their way through grief; emotion is their pilot. So often men say they have no words to grieve with, and they describe themselves as mute. It is as if men lack a universal language to convey their feelings or clothe their experiences. They feel paralyzed. Women seem unable to get beyond their feelings. Grief overshadows their life. Many confide that they long to end the tears and, in fact, feel envious that men so easily jump to action and go about the daily business of life.

The incongruity between men's and women's ways of grieving clearly takes its toll on relationships. Divorce, separation, and marital discord are extremely high among those who have experienced loss and grief. Most women sincerely want to break through to their partner, to know what, if anything, is in his heart. Most men also concede that they want to stop the charades and for once feel understood in their grief. All of us have the right to grieve for as long and as hard as we need to. Through our intimate connection with our partner, we have a place where we can find genuine support, validate our feelings, and give each other permission to grieve in our own way and according to our own timetable.

Concentrate on the possibilities

Men and women can walk together in their sorrow. As intimates, we can begin to understand each other more fully. When women concentrate on all the possible ways there are to grieve, they can be witness to their partner's courage. They can experience their significant other's despair, not just shudder at his anger or rage. If we approach our grief as intimate partners, our awareness becomes infused with respect, empathy, understanding, and trust. Like a glowing polestar in the night heavens, these values can help guide us past our doubts and fears and lead us beyond the restrictions our expectations and prejudices place on us. Our intimate bond rewards us with an appreciation of our uniqueness and a sense of good fortune for the strengths each partner brings to the journey through grief.

When women concentrate on the possibilities in their relationship, they expand their potential for healing. Through a new understanding, they gain strength and hopefulness to combat the burdens and desolation of grief. Grieving is a horrendous experience made even worse when intimate relationships fall short and the comfort and support so badly needed is absent. Opening one's mind to other possibilities will allow intimacy to grow.

Grief has no claim on gender. Men do grieve. A child's suicide, the onset of dementia in a parent, an impending job loss are all life-shattering events. Though their feelings and words may seem incongruent to many women, men experience a level of anguish and desperation that mirrors that of women. The fact that many men choose not to talk about their feelings does not mean that they don't have feelings, but rather that they don't have the words to express their feelings in the face of senseless and incomprehensible tragedy. Men are in a double bind. We ask them to honor the masculine code by protecting and defending, yet we also demand that they be tender and sensitive. We tell boys to let mama kiss their hurts away, yet chide them for not being tougher when taunted or teased by friends or siblings. Too often, they are caught in the middle.

Through our love and concern for one another, we find the courage, patience, and compassion to recognize and respect our common pain. Mutuality encourages us to set each other free to grieve in our own way and at our own pace. It enables us to provide genuine support in a way that does not constrict, enable, or create dependency. Grief ought not to be a point of division, but of connection.

2

The Language of Grief

Each tear burns out my eyes,
Mocking my resolve.
I want to take my thumb and
Shove them back inside.
I struggle for a blank expression,
A fleshy facade I've seen before
Staring in every morning mirror.
I invent silence with a broken tongue.

—Louis Cerulli

My Father

"You have known for five months that the sports editor's position was vacant. Why did you decide to apply for the job now?" asked one of the newspaper editors interviewing me.

I explained that five months before, my wife, Patrice, was expecting our first child and we were still settling into life in our new house. I had felt confident I could make the move from a staff sportswriter to the sports editor, but I believed the changes and subsequent stresses would be too many and too great.

I started to say that my father had died four months before the position was advertised. When I mentioned my father's death to the editors' team, though, I could no longer speak.

The words of explanation would not come. They stuck deep in my throat. I coughed, as if that would lodge the words free. Tears welled in my eyes. My heart accelerated. I looked at the five editors sitting at the table, hoping for assistance. I wanted to tell them that five months ago, I did not feel ready for the challenges of a new job. I wanted to tell them that when the job first opened, I was still grieving.

My interview was coming unhinged—because I loved my father and he was no longer around.

I had not anticipated my reaction—my inability to speak the words in my head.

I can still see my dad in the hospital bed the day he died. Surrounding him were the hospital chaplain, his pastor from home, and his family—my mother, my wife, and me. At age eighty-one, my father could not overcome the sudden and dramatic effects of Wagener's vasculitis, a rare disease that tormented his kidneys, lungs, and blood vessels. He died two days before Christmas in 1996.

Just after he died, my mother leaned forward and kissed my father on the forehead. She ran her hand through his soft, white hair, and told him how much she loved him. "I miss him already," she said.

Soon after my father died, a snowstorm struck. It seemed appropriate because he was born on a snowy February day. He loved winter months—chopping wood, shoveling snow, and walking in the woods. He had requested that "Winter Wonderland" be played at his memorial service, and, as if on cue, his service was marked by falling snow.

My father, Frank, was aptly named. His directness could make the more "politically correct" cringe. There was "right" and there was "wrong" for my father, a man who spent much of his law-and-order career as a police juvenile officer. Honesty and integrity were his benchmarks. He was stern, but fair.

After my father's death, vivid memories came into my mind all the time.

When I was a young child, he cut my hair. The crew cut and the bowl cut were his specialties. He told me to eat my peas, all four of those despicable creatures that I had scattered around my plate. Once he suggested that I try a new dessert treat he had made for the two of us—a cantaloupe malt. He defended me when I was wronged. He asked me what I had learned in school. He threw the baseball to me—sometimes high, sometimes low, sometimes in the dirt—so I might be a good fielding first baseman.

When I was a teenager, I once called him after I locked the keys in the car at a Milwaukee Brewers' baseball game at Milwaukee County Stadium. He did not yell, but drove the twenty minutes from our home to the stadium and took my high school friend and me out to eat after the game. When I listened to the radio in the car, pop tunes blaring loudly, he would say, "And they call this music?" I remember how he hurried home from church on Sundays so he would not miss the kickoff to the Green Bay Packers' game.

Just two days before he died, my father wondered if my wife and I had an attorney read over the transaction for our house purchase. His mind was keen, but his body was failing. He knew he would not be with my mother anymore. They had been married forty-five years. He knew he would not be alive when my first child was born.

My father's death is hard for me. He is not around to answer the questions I have. He is not around to share in my accomplishments. He is not here to provide love and support.

It should have been no surprise to me that when I began to talk about my father during my job interview, my voice cracked with emotion and I could not speak.

It is easier for me to write about my father's death than it is to talk about it. After all, writing is what I do for my work. Writing is my way of expressing the feelings pent-up inside. The task still is daunting and not without tears.

My tears do come. Sometimes, they come at the computer keyboard. Sometimes, they come while I'm driving the car and hearing those pop songs on the radio "they call music," or while looking at my daughter, Gabrielle, in her car seat. Sometimes, they come when I go alone and talk to him at his grave site.

Sometimes, the tears start to come and my voice chokes when I say his name during a job interview.

I felt embarrassed during that interview. I apologized to the others. This, I believed, was not appropriate behavior in such a *setting. I was not strong. I was emotional. I made the interviewers uncomfortable, I thought. I responded differently—wrongly—from the way a man is "supposed" to react to grief.*

However, my interviewers—my colleagues—did not share my view. Later, after my embarrassment subsided, it was easier for me to agree with how they saw the situation.

I am human.

I loved my father.

I missed him then.

I still do.

—Jon Masson

Language. It defines our life by lending concrete shape to our experiences. Our thoughts, emotions, and actions are mere abstractions without words to clothe them and make them recognizable, identifiable, and valid. Words, and the pictures that rise from them, give us meaning and enable us to communicate—sometimes well, sometimes not so well—with one another. Language delineates our reality and gives voice to our own personal story, our unique history. Language constructs our world view and our ability to verbalize what we know, what we experience, and what we do. Words are anchors that integrate thoughts and emotions. Language puts the motion in emotion.

All of us learned to construct words and language from our interactions with others. Babies begin to name things by grunts and gestures. Later, sounds and words form through imitation, practice, and reinforcement. The vocabulary we use is based on our experiences of the world and what specific words were used to define, categorize, and make sense of these events.

Much has been written about differences in feminine and masculine language. Most of us notice these variances in vocabulary and word choice, and also in comprehension and the specific meaning one attaches to a particular word. It is not uncommon for the genders to complain about differences in such common words as *trust, safety, honesty, love, intimacy,* or *sensitiveness.* Feminine language is often described as intuitive, earthy, fluid, or elusive, whereas masculine language is thought to be orderly, concise, controlling, and goal-oriented.

Women largely focus on connections and interdependence in their language. They seem very concerned about their internal world and use words to explore and to understand their emotions. That's why women tend to talk about their feelings of grief, and talk and talk and talk some more. Men's language, on the other hand, is often an exercise in power and independence. Men appear to be more interested in the external world around them, and they rely on words to maintain their status and personal freedom. Busy with the outside world, men tend to ignore or devalue emotional issues.

Men may be silent about emotional issues not only because they devalue them, but because they are unable to talk about them. Ask a man about the death of his child, his war experience, or a serious accident on the job, and he will likely protest that he has "no words." Others might attempt to explain and then in mid-sentence say they "can't speak." It is not an inability to talk, to produce words, nor is it a fumbling for just the right words. Men lack a *language for grief.* They have no ready phrases, terms, statements, or cliches. When trying to describe their experience of anguish, sorrow, or deep pain, many men simply come up empty-handed.

To say that men are unable to describe their emotions is not to say that men lack feelings. On the contrary, Jon Masson's story and all the personal stories found in this book are irrefutable evidence of men's deep emotions. Emotions are genderless. They are as central to our life as air. Emotional responses such as "fight or flight" have helped our species survive. Emotions define our relationships with others and with ourselves. Without emotions, we—both men and women— would be powerless and helpless. Men have emotions; they simply respond to and describe them differently than females do.

Women tend to have a rich and fluid language for grief. Many women can draw from a large reservoir of personal sensitivities to create authentic narratives of their pain. Their words and phrases bring to light all that is felt and experienced, whether painful, foreboding, hopeful, or horrifying. When an emotion is felt, a woman is more likely than a man to be able to put a name to it. Women have neither more nor fewer feelings than men. What they do have is a prescribed and effective set of words to give meaning and flesh to their emotional experiences, and, perhaps even more importantly, the permission to do so.

Men as a whole have not created a language of grief for themselves. Men have been raised mute, silent to their emotional pain. Men know that such words exist; they hear them from women, read them in books, and see them in dictionaries. But the words are not to be found in the male thesaurus. Words of grief are hollow inscriptions on granite headstones or glossy white sympathy cards. Most men don't own words to convey their grief.

Cultural pressures work to make males into "true men." Boys are taught to be strong, outspoken, and intrepid individuals, proud to bear the mantle of masculinity. Fathers, mentors, and peers define and confirm the boys' masculinity and instruct them to be independent, fearless, self-assured, and powerful. At the same time, men impress upon boys that vulnerability, tenderness, and sensitivity are weaknesses for the male gender. They give boys no names for their very real and felt emotions, and no permission to express them. Through men's examples, boys learn to segment their feelings and conceal them from view.

Over and over, boys are ridiculed or punished when they appear weak, sickly, or unmanly in the eyes of men or other male peers. In both spoken and unspoken ways, they are taught to deny or abandon those parts of their identity that dare feel pain, whether emotional, spiritual, or physical. Youngsters are told that a tumble off a bike and a scraped knee "is nothing." Later, as teens, the experience is reinforced when a young man is ordered back on the field after a defensive back topples him on a pass, tearing ligaments in his shoulder. Like the mythological hero Hercules, boys are expected to endure and persevere no matter how painful or difficult the task. The message is clear. There is honor in denying pain, but not in feeling pain.

Boys are taught to see life as a hierarchy. Groomed to seek status, they engage in activities that reinforce their rank or position in the world. The games they play as children have leaders who give orders and make demands. Their games have winners and losers, champions and failures. Boys are not to have emotional feelings about winning or losing, but to think of these things logically. One is either one up or one down. Boys argue and challenge each other directly. But arguments are not about hurt feelings, disappointment, or other such emotional issues. They are about skill, status, control, rules. Once again, boys learn that feelings have neither merit nor a place in their vocabulary.

The experiences of girls are traditionally very different. Girls are often taught to connect feelings to real events, sensations, and thoughts. Mothers, teachers, and peers encourage girls to develop an emotional language as a way to identify, sort, label, and make meaning of their world. They laud girls' tenderness, sensitivity, and compassion and make much of their ability to be sympathetic and understanding friends. It's not surprising, then, that girls are less apt than boys to play in large groups, often preferring pairs, or even small, intimate groups.

Becoming skillful is important for girls, but they tend to be less interested than boys in status and competition. Girls like challenges and having control, but not at the expense of losing friendships, appearing "bossy," or being disliked. They are taught to lead not with demands and orders, but by

encouraging, supporting, and nurturing cooperation and connectedness. Emotions and maintaining a sense of harmony in
relationships are at issue during arguments and conflicts. For
many women, life begins and ends with emotions.

Men do not rely as much on emotions to shape their life.
Their lack of a language of grief is a testament to this fact. Yet
if emotions such as anguish, sorrow, distress, regret, or sadness
are not named or validated, they remain in an eerie, frightening
void. The male may be unable to connect his internal experience or turmoil to the external world. No matter what disappointments, horrors, or trauma he experiences, he may be
unable to speak about such things. And his silence may threaten
to disconnect him from reality.

Feelings are not illusory. Nor can they be casually dismissed by culturally dominant notions of manhood or even by
unrelenting peer pressure. Men cannot shake off, outrun, or
outmaneuver their feelings. This is what Jon discovered during
his job interview. Not to be denied, feelings find a way of overpowering men and expressing themselves, directly or indirectly.
A man may become perfectionistic about the way his lawn looks
or obsessed with athletic exercise like running or jogging. His
inner world has found a way to drive and to control his outer
world, and he doesn't know it.

Grief comes to men like a live electric current. It's like
plunging a fork in an electric toaster. The jolt is so jarring
that men are forced, at least momentarily, to touch that deep,
frightening void of numb and unspoken feelings. The discomfort is so immense, the man has no choice but to deal with it.
Many believe they have amputated that part of themselves and
so become confused and troubled. Still, many men are reluctant to risk being labeled a weeper or fool, and are

embarrassed to show, let alone talk about, their emotions. You won't often see a man cry on someone's shoulder. Without a language of grief, a man will attempt to gloss over his feelings. In doing so, he will have no opportunity to reveal himself, thereby diminishing his capacity to heal.

Men can become prisoners of their own experiences. Taught to adhere strictly to a narrow range of behaviors, conditions, and elements befitting their gender, men can come to believe that they lack permission to do the work of grieving. Grief is reduced to a rather perfunctory, controllable matter. Many men move decisively and swiftly in grief, believing this is not the time to be self-indulgent. Rather, they see grief as a time to exhibit courage and bravery and maintain dignity and decorum.

Grief is inescapable. No one chooses to have their newborn son die, to lose the job they devoted ten years of their life to, or to have their bank account run dry because of a catastrophic illness. Had we options, we would certainly trade everything to have our old life back, but grief doesn't give us a choice about what life will bring. In order to survive, we must deal with the havoc and devastation that has been visited on both our external and internal worlds. We need to make sense of what has happened to our life and our soul. Since our inner world defines our outer world, this is where we all must begin.

We live in a verbal society. Words have tremendous power to communicate our desires, hopes, and expectations. They structure our reality and define our intimacy. Through language we communicate our immediate experiences and felt emotions. When words accurately connect with a felt sensation, we achieve "authenticity"—something women often believe is missing when men grieve.

An authentic voice names what is true. To some extent, authenticity neutralizes gender. All of us know that there are many times when both women and men agree upon the meaning of an experience or situation. But, in grief, the words men and women use to describe their common experiences can seem radically different, if they exist at all. The vagueness and ambiguity that men often exhibit about their emotions can infuriate women. Women know that there are words for grief, and they cannot understand why men are so unwilling to use them. It does not always occur to them that their partner may not know this language as well as they do.

Listen with a new ear

Instead of focusing on what is absent, women can listen for what is present in their communications and interactions with their partner. To move beyond frustration and closer to understanding, women need a new ear, an ear that is tuned to men's unspoken words. Many women understand the intuitive and relational words of grief—words that are ripe for the picking, bursting with immediate meaning. Far fewer women understand silence, or what may lie behind the silence.

Listening with a new and different ear, a woman can have access to the silence. Within this silence she may discover references to other experiences, situations, and events clothed in brazen, aggressive metaphors or phrases. These metaphors and phrases may point to catastrophe and devastation, to things that are irreversible, ultimate, and permanent. Hidden in these metaphors and phrases may be clues to her partner's grief—the long shadows cast by his nearly invisible pain. She may also discover more generalized references to what has been lost: a house now quiet, clothes no longer worn, memories of times past, or activities once enjoyed. What is in the silence is the truth. Men do feel.

Men may have to learn a new language or reconstruct their current language to be authentic in their grief. Women, by themselves, cannot supply this language or define men's truth. By listening, acknowledging, and being empathetic to men's dilemmas, though, women can join men on their journey.

3

The Process of Grieving: The Thinking Male

I wrap myself in tattered
Proverbs that let the wind
Cut through the skin. I search for
A mother in hollow bones, draped
In wrinkled tissue, cold in a box.
She hangs in my mind,
An ache which ebbs as it ages,
A memory balanced on a memory.

—Louis Cerulli

No Longer Here

*I can't remember how long it took me to become aware that my
mother was dying. On one holiday visit she was her normal self,
but by the next visit it was as if the life had been drained from
her. My mother suffered from adult-onset diabetes. Each time I
would take the long trip back to my hometown, I saw my mother
lose more and more of her normal functioning. For four or five
years, I feared that every visit could be the last time I would see
her. After she sustained a heart attack, doctors told us that she
had suffered a series of small strokes. The diabetes, coupled with
the strokes, was slowly killing her.*

*A large part of my experience in my mother's dying process
was as an observer. I watched her gradually become completely
dependent upon my father's care. My parents had switched
roles, with my father now assuming the household chores. In
addition, my dad had become a twenty-four-hour nurse for my
mother. He prepared meals, monitored blood sugar levels, and
gave insulin injections.*

*In the last two years before her death, my mother deterio-
rated to the point where she couldn't move by herself. Her speech
was severely slurred. Physically, she was an invalid, but it was
obvious that her mind was still sharp. The idea of an adult
becoming so horribly dependent was like a nightmare to me, yet I
was forced to watch. This was my mother, and I was determined
to see past the sickness to the woman I loved and deeply
admired. But the illness whittled away at her, taking her from me
one small piece at a time.*

*The last time I saw my mother, her helplessness was com-
plete. She could not speak, and her movement was limited and
erratic. She behaved like a toddler. When you turned away from*

her, she would knock something over or cause some kind of trou-ble to get your attention. However, I began to view her helpless-ness in a different light. The intimacy that had developed between my mother and father was touching, and in some ways my mother seemed to be enjoying herself. She remained an inte-gral part of the family in spite of her limited physical participa-tion. My family revolved around her as if she were a new baby. My mother was leaving this life the way she entered it—as a well-cared-for infant. I began to see how being helpless was not the worst possible thing that could happen to a person. But even the little pleasures I saw her experiencing could not clear away my gut-wrenching emotions.

Throughout my mother's illness, I fantasized that her death would come as a relief. I was wrong. In fact, her death was so painful that it was difficult to find words to describe the feelings. Physically, I felt as if I had been kicked in the chest. I felt like a ship whose anchor had been cut, and now I was floating aim-lessly. I must have seemed like a manic-depressive. One moment I was blissful at the thought that my mother had become one with the universe and I could feel her presence in the birds and trees. The next moment I felt like I had survived a holocaust, and the world was devoid of any meaning other then loss and suffering.

Now that a year has passed since her death, I have moments when I can think of my mother without being thrown into an emotional tailspin. Because I think of her so much, she seems in some ways more present to me now than when she was alive. I am constantly reminded of her, but these recollections are not as painful as they used to be. I can't say exactly when the pain receded, but it did.

Sometimes, out of nowhere, the pain returns, and I suspect it will continue to do so for the rest of my life. When I'm feeling this extreme loss, I realize that the price of remembering my mother comes with the cold reality that she is simply "no longer here." There are no religious or philosophical explanations to help me understand the pure experience of her utter and complete absence from my life.

—Jim Amundsen

The notion that grieving is a process is familiar to most of us. There is a method and a forward, progressive, or continuous movement toward a goal or end state. Often we talk about grief as an active rather than a passive process. Grieving is not something done to us, but rather something we do. Thus, grief demands a response from us, one other than resignation. An active process specifies choices and presumes change. More than anything, the process of grief is about transformation.

To process something implies time, effort, preparation, patience, persistence. Typically, working through a process or bringing it to conclusion requires steps or tasks. Time must be set aside, effort expended, preparations made, and patience and persistence must rule the day. In grief, we know that it's not the ticking of the clock that moves us in the process, but what we do with the time. Our efforts measure more than how much better we feel now; they also take into account how often we feel bad. Growth, victories, and healing are never that obvious in grief, and hindsight is likely better than foresight. We witness progress in our grieving by looking back, instead of looking forward.

The act of grieving is an intrusion on our physical, emotional, social, spiritual, and cognitive worlds. We hurt physically: shoulders, chest, arms, legs, head. We are a jumble of emotions, and our heart feels trampled and irreparable. Our social connections have been severed; we've lost our place in the scheme of things. We wonder about God, and question our faith and beliefs. We are filled with irrational thoughts and wonder if we've truly gone crazy. Many of us are left wondering if we can really deal with this thing called grief.

Our attitudes and behaviors take a roller coaster ride when we are grieving. Previous patterns of eating, sleeping, and daily living no longer make any sense. We feel numb to the normal activities that once gave us pleasure and kept us going from day to day. We cruise on automatic pilot, unable to concentrate or keep on task. We desperately want the world to stop so we can get off, but the world seems indifferent to our needs.

Among our natural reactions to grief are shock, numbness, anger, denial, disbelief, disorientation, and despair. We vigorously protest the loss and attempt to recover what we once had. At the heart of our grief is an intense desire to have our job back, our partner back, our life back. Life is a mess, and it's difficult, if not impossible, to imagine getting on with living. The chances that we might ever heal and be whole again seem extremely remote. It is as if the sun has been eclipsed, and we live in the penumbra of loss.

Grieving is not a linear process. People don't just plow ahead and then dust their hands off and announce that they are done with *that* piece of work. No, grieving is circular and repetitive. We cycle through grief over and over; it's the old "two steps forward, one backward." We make progress, advance forward, then we backtrack, retracing our steps. Grieving isn't continuous, but it is recurring. Events like anniversaries, holidays, or new losses trigger our grief. Before we know it, we are grieving again. We never get over our loss, we just get through it. For good or bad, grief dictates that we are never quite the same again.

Grief is work—intense work. The lessons that grief teaches us are not for the skittish, the weak, or the avoiders. Grieving means coming to accept what has happened in our life. As most of us know, this task is tremendously difficult and onerous. But over time we must untie the bonds of our lost relationship and slowly let reality seep into our consciousness. The finality of the death or tragic event must become evident to us, and we must find acceptance without losing our soul.

Ultimately, we must experience the pain of grief, and not just in a cursory fashion. Grief demands that we struggle with our feelings, fully and completely. Those who hide their pain or try to ignore it only intensify it over time. By releasing our pain, we make room for healing. The tears, cries, anguish, frustration, and desperation must be acknowledged so that the healing process can begin.

Grief creates chaos. Like a glass plate dropped on a kitchen floor, our life is fractured by grief. We must change, adapt, reconstruct our world, and fit the loss into a new reality. As anguishing and awful as it seems, the world has drastically changed for us, and we must learn that we cannot possibly recapture what we once had. It is up to us to find new meaning for our life.

The ways people cope with grief are as distinct as the blades of grass that grow across the prairie. These distinctions are most marked between men and women. Grief and grieving are centered in our emotional lives; aspects of which are developmentally unique to each gender. Men are taught to be less self-disclosing, less expressive, and less interdependent. Women, on the other hand, are encouraged to focus on affiliation, connectedness, and intimacy. Women not only desire expressiveness, they need to express their feelings. Men's inexpressive tendencies cause conflict. It is as if the genders are at cross-purposes.

The emotional domain of many men tends to be relatively narrow. They are fearful of the consequences, culturally and personally, of expressing their emotions. No one wants to be held in contempt, humiliated, or ridiculed at the water cooler for behaviors deemed unmanly. Suppression is not a case of being either unable or unwilling to express feelings; it is both. The absence of a language to describe men's inner world compounds the issue even more. Men do not express themselves in the same vocabulary that women use.

Men tend to distrust their feelings. Many fear that if they begin to let their feelings out, they might not be able to shut them off. This can be a terrifying and repugnant thought. While women sometimes worry about this, too, their level of anxiety is not nearly as acute. By viewing emotions as uncontrollable and volatile, men reinforce their belief that it's safer to keep feelings concealed. Because men are given little encouragement to express their emotions, they are hesitant to expose any emotional vulnerability.

Intimacy is dangerous territory for many men. It threatens their freedom and the protective walls of silence they sometimes build around themselves. Men tend to form close friendships less on the basis of affiliation or intimacy than on the basis of shared activities. Men worry that intimacy may overwhelm them with intense emotions and draw them into risky interconnections. Unlike women, the bonds they form usually have more to do with loyalty than shared feelings, and they tend to be less self-disclosing than women, particularly about their emotions and most private feelings.

Generally speaking, men bond with other men to confirm their status and competency in the world. Friendships are the basis for mutual rivalries and personal challenge. When feelings come up, many men change the subject, downplay the issue, or deflect the topic away from themselves. These men prefer to act as if everything is fine, as if some things are better left unsaid. They maintain a strict code of silence and refuse to cross certain boundaries. Even those men who are dissatisfied with this state of affairs, though, may have no idea how to change it.

Women find their place in the world through relationships. A woman's ability to form friendships and intimate bonds is at the core of her identity. These relationships enable women to express their hurts, disappointments, and pain, and to be supported and encouraged. Women feel their way through grief. While grieving, they are able to disclose their most intimate feelings—for example, the guilt they feel for surviving a loved one or for failing to prevent a death or loss. Unlike men, women seek and expect to find a safe venue for expressing what is in their heart and soul.

Men are supposed to be a rock; they are supposed to be the protector and problem-solver for their family. Men are rarely presented with an alternative to being strong, capable, and in control. There is a widespread expectation that men should manage and moderate family grief. They are to insulate the family from further harm and take responsibility and repair what has happened. Of course, it is impossible to put things back exactly the way they were before, but the urge to do so is so strong and the expectation so great that many men work furiously to do just that. They search feverishly for ways to mend their family, insisting that things will soon return to normal. Like the white knights of olden times, men are the rescuers who will restore and preserve family unity. To carry out this role, men are forced to postpone or even suppress their own grief. The pressures are unrelenting.

Grieving is about feelings, and many men know this perfectly well. After years of suppressing, repressing, and denying one's emotions, grief momentarily strips away all defenses. Jim Amundsen's story shows how pained he was by his mother's illness and death. Men are not immune to feelings; grief affects them as strongly as it does women. But their process of grieving is often less visible than women's. Men grieve on the inside, and their grief work tends to be more cognitive than emotional.

That men *think* their way through grief is something many women know quite well. They often see men metaphorically storing their grief in a file drawer in the back of their brain. Men seem to be running away, to have dismissed and locked away their feelings. To do the same, women feel as if they would have to cut out part of their heart. Women want an intimate connection with their partners, but, when their partners pull away, they have no way to break through to see if their partners are actively grieving.

Men often try to block out their grief. Some make a conscious effort not to think about the death of their loved one, the job loss, the impending divorce, or the feelings associated with these events. Their efforts are deliberate attempts to keep the negative and painful from penetrating their soul. To do this, men may intentionally think about practical and routine things, like work, sports, or household chores. This sort of self-distraction keeps distressing thoughts and memories under control and, at least for a time, gives men some emotional relief. To drift in and out of their grief gives men the sense that they are working through it, letting go whenever and however they can.

Men feel pressured to be productive citizens and responsible family men. They have to be busy doing things and demonstrating their competence. Activity is a natural way for men to escape trauma. Keeping busy has value for men; it consumes their energy and time, and keeps their mind occupied. Some men seem to get obsessive about such things as work, exercise, health, sports, parenting, or domestic chores. Many lose themselves in the safety of work and career and become workaholics. Others take on addictions like alcohol, gambling, or sex; some even become hyper-spiritual. Compartmentalizing and distracting their feelings helps men avoid their pain.

More than a few men turn to physical activities as a way to keep distracted. Cutting a cord of firewood or building a storage shed allows physical pain and mental concentration to displace grief. Any activity will do as long as it keeps the man busy and helps him ignore his pain. The physical work becomes another way to escape reality.

Women often criticize men for intellectualizing their grief. It's just a way for men to hide their feelings, they believe. From the woman's viewpoint, there is a disconnection between the head and the heart. The man's attempt to "stay in his head" is an effort at rationalizing what has happened to him. By systematically reviewing events and circumstances, the man is searching for a logical and reasonable explanation. He believes that one exists; to discover it, he just has to think hard or long enough. Searching out information, studying the literature, or getting the advice of others fuels his thinking. Intellectualizing does not deter the man's painful memories. Rather, he tolerates these memories in order to get the facts right and to see if there is some detail he has missed. Uncomfortable as these memories are, he knows they are key to his thought process.

There is no denying that grief is a very private experience. Sometimes women, just like men, would rather be alone with their feelings. But, more often than not, women seek companionship to support their feelings and to satisfy their needs for intimacy. Men hurt and know they hurt, but they prefer to cope alone. Whether on the job when no one is around, out in the woods, in a boat, driving alone in the car, or outside in the garage, men find private places and times to express their emotions. Men use these private moments to unleash their pent-up feelings and to confront their emotions. Men do cry, but rarely around others. Male conditioning would have it no other way.

Grief is the great emasculator. Most of us will know no other time in our life when we have been so absolutely and completely stripped of control. This insecurity is especially intense for men whose identity, worth, and self-esteem are tied closely to issues of power and authority. Not only must these men maintain self-control, they must be masters of their domain. To be seen as helpless and fearful—or worse, a failure—would be humiliating. Rather than being defeated by their loss, many men charge ahead, looking for ways to demonstrate their control over it. For some men, this may mean engaging in activities related directly to the loss, like taking charge of funeral arrangements or pursuing legal remedies. Some focus on other aspects of life, like cleaning out the basement or tending the garden. Men rail against powerlessness. Their efforts to exert influence publicly demonstrate that they have not lost their ability to make decisions or bring order to a disordered state. Failure is not a reasonable option.

Lead with trust

As we have seen, grief and grieving pose serious threats to our self-identity. It is easy to lose oneself in grief. Those who treat grief passively fail to realize its potency. Grief comes to us without choice. None of us asks to be dismissed from a job, suffer a miscarriage, or be injured in a serious car accident. Yet how we deal with the grieving process always involves choice. Most women approach the work of grieving by actively expressing their emotional turmoil. Their expressiveness is visible. Men know when women grieve. Men's grief, on the other hand, is often invisible to women.

Women must lead with trust, approaching men and grief with openness, not suspicion. The choices men make about processing their grief may not be self-evident, but more than one path can lead to the same destination. Men's grief is cognitive. Though largely inexpressive, men do find ways to express their feelings. Men want to be alone with their grief and will create or structure time to deal with accumulated feelings. These are things women must trust with an open mind and heart.

Most women believe that the healthiest way to cope with grief is to express their feelings. This is why women insist, beg, manipulate, and cajole their partners. How men grieve does not look "normal" or "right" to most women. From a woman's perspective, it does not look as if it works, either. But it is not reasonable for women to force men to grieve as they do. With an open mind, women can move beyond what seems "normal." They can come to understand and support what men are doing.

PART TWO

REALITIES AND CHALLENGES

4

Denial

I look at you in miniature.
There's another face inside the one you're wearing,
Subtle along a whiskerline,
Pinched in your brow,
And all your gray ripped from socket.
I grew up with that phantom,
Face within a face.
I see what I want to see.

—Louis Cerulli

The Last Fishing Trip

My brother was diagnosed with cancer.

We had not been close for many years, but I have memories of us as children walking all over town collecting matchbook covers. We did all those senseless things that mean so much, like digging holes and building forts in our backyard. Perhaps our most important treasure was our tree house. It stood in our parent's lot, but it was like a second home just for us.

As Mark and I grew older, we began to spend less time together. We had gone from best friends to distant "family members." Even though it was time for us to start developing our own unique personalities, I regret not taking our close childhood ties into later life. It was even more poignant when the cancer had taken control of Mark, and his condition was terminal.

Mark had suffered from mental illness and alcoholism. He had always been a sensitive, artistic individual, and I guess I was in denial about his illness. I found it hard to be with him, blaming our time apart on my marriage and job. Meanwhile, Mark was undergoing shock treatments and therapy. Our relationship as kids had a real reciprocity and spontaneity, and now I looked at him as someone I hardly knew.

My brother learned that he had terminal cancer at age forty-seven. It seemed hypocritical suddenly to spend more time with him after so many years of denying our relationship. The reality was that Mark needed extra attention, which often took the form of transportation to his chemotherapy treatments. So I decided not to worry about hypocrisy and took on the duties of helping to care for Mark.

Consciously, I agreed to drive Mark to chemotherapy out of obligation, but perhaps I was hoping to reignite the close relationship we had when we were young. I began to take Mark to treatment every other time he needed it, alternating treatments with my sister Karol. Two to three times a week, Mark and I had time to spend together in the car.

I wove stories together as the worn-out scenery of our trip to the hospital passed outside the window. I tried to get him to talk and to reach deep inside his memory for the bond we had as kids. It was frustrating when these attempts at conversation didn't yield much. Then, on one trip to the hospital, I asked, "Where would you like to go besides treatment?" He looked as if he wanted to say something and paused. So I asked the question differently, "If you could go anywhere in the world, where would you like to go?" Strangely, something inside me seemed to give way, and I finally began to realize that my brother was really going to die. I was prepared to take him to Europe or anywhere he'd read about. I figured I'd do anything for him now. The costs would be dealt with later.

"Where do you want to go?" I asked him again. He wanted to go fishing on one of the lakes our Grandpa had fished with us as children. This seemed like an ideal setting to resurrect some of the camaraderie we had shared as kids. We planned to go fishing the next day, and I spent the evening with Mark bustling around, assembling the tackle. It felt just like the night before a fishing trip when we were kids, and I was full of anticipation. Even though Mark merely watched most of the preparation, I felt as if he were excited about the journey as well.

The day of our trip, it occurred to me that we did not have fishing licenses. After digging worms the way we had years before as children, we stopped in a bait store to get the licenses. The sign in the bait store declared $10.00 for one day and $17.00 for a season pass. I balked at buying a one-day license. I didn't want to admit to myself that Mark wouldn't be around long enough to fish again. It wasn't fair that I was finally willing to face my pain and then have to lose Mark to his disease. I looked into my brother's eyes and then put $34.00 on the counter.

Grandpa Meline's lake was like a sheet of glass with our rental boat in the center. The reflections of the rising sun tinted our breath, making it vaguely visible in the chill of the morning air. I baited one of the drop lines Mark had prepared just like when we fished as kids. Mark was nodding off, his head fighting a losing battle to remain erect. I pretended that he was just sleepy that it wasn't the disease that made him weak. I woke him up and helped him get a worm on his hook so we could fish.

After sitting in silence for some time, I felt a tiny tug on the end of my line. Remembering all the training Grandpa Meline had given me, I hooked the fish! The next few minutes were critical as I alternately gave line and pulled in. As the fish emerged in a frenzy of twisting and splashing, I turned toward Mark and found him asleep again.

The rest of the afternoon was like that. I would catch something and find my brother dozing. My brother wanted to fish, but I was the only one alert enough to actually do it. Finally, I resigned myself to making sure my weary brother didn't fall out of the boat. The cancer wouldn't allow us to have the kind of fishing trip we'd had when we were little, but at least we were together. Each moment was a gift, even if it didn't happen in the way I expected.

On the way back home I wondered how much Mark had enjoyed himself. So I asked him, "What did you think of our fishing trip?" With the biggest smile I'd seen in years, he said, "Oh, it was just great to sit in the boat and feel the wind blowing on my *body." That moment was worth a million dollars to me. One fishing trip couldn't replace all those years we had lost, but it confirmed the love we still had as brothers.*

Shortly after our fishing trip Mark got too sick to be moved, and a few months later he died. We never used the season passes.

—Larry D. Johnson

Reality is the here-and-now. Sometimes, it is pleasant, even joyous. We can like what we are doing, how our life is going, the plans or activities we have for the day. When reality is good, we don't give it a second thought. But reality can also be unpleasant, even disastrous; and life can suddenly feel cruel or heartless. A death, physical illness, or a job loss can drastically impact our cozy sense of reality. Reality suddenly demands a second thought—and much more.

Reality is tenacious; it refuses to be ignored. When we are grieving, reminders of our loved one or of what we once had are all too visible and painful—a song, a favorite food, a familiar image, a word or phrase. Most of us prefer to test reality slowly and on our own terms. We know rationally that a time will come when we must face the truth, when we must accept that the past cannot be changed. But until our heart catches up to our mind, we don't want this time to come. The horrifying and startling news of our personal tragedy is more than we can handle. To mediate that information, most of us psychologically withdraw and wrap ourselves in a protective coat of denial.

Initially, we often feel immobilized by death or loss. Things feel a blur, as if time were standing still. Many women complain of feeling paralyzed, unable to sort out their feelings or even to communicate effectively. Their cries and weeping are a kind of vocalized shield intended to block out reality. Grieving gives women a sense of being engulfed, almost smothered, by riotous emotions. They want support and some assurance that the pain will not last forever. More comfortable talking out their pain, women struggle with where to begin in describing the enormity of their sorrow.

Grief immobilizes men, too. The reality of what has occurred shatters their sense of a controlled and orderly life.

Dazed and defenseless, they feel ill-prepared for what lies ahead. If only someone would outline the steps or draw a schematic, then they might know what to do. Feelings of panic and insecurity are frightening and even degrading. Many men are unsure where to turn or how to preserve their masculinity.

Anxiety is a constant companion for many grieving men and women. Grief brings such a tremendous sense of danger to our lives. It is not so much a sense of impending doom as it is the pervasive sense that we are no longer safe. The world has dealt us a blow, and we no longer feel as trusting about our place in the universe. Old rules about the fairness of life no longer hold true. It is as if we are at the mercy of the great unknown, and some of us are left wondering when the next tragedy will strike.

Anxiety has a way of making us feel defenseless and vulnerable. It can reduce us to a state of helplessness. Overwhelmed, emotionally bruised and battered, many of us choose denial as a way to isolate ourselves and withdraw. Anxiety has gripped us so tightly that we can only stare straight ahead, unresponsive to others, or thrust our hands deep in our pockets and pace an endless pattern on the floor. We are scared. Grieving hurts, and often we're too numb to interact with others. Our preoccupation with what has happened may mean that we need to limit the amount of stimulation in our life. Withdrawing will give us a little breathing room. Pulling into ourselves and shutting the world out may seem the only rational way to keep sane. In the early days of grieving, denial keeps us insulated and safeguarded until we are better able to deal with our thoughts and emotions.

At one time or another, most men and women have been in denial about something in their life. Perhaps it was about a poor report card, a spurned lover, or a driving violation they felt they did not deserve. Denial is our attempt to modify or reject reality—those things that we do not believe, agree to, or want. Women tend to see denial as the principal way men cope with grief. In contrast, they see themselves as more confrontational, as more willing to process their feelings and take an active role in moving through their grief. While it may be true that men, more than women, reject grief by denying their feelings of anguish, emptiness, sorrow, despair, and hopelessness, women also use denial to protect their own vulnerabilities and to regulate their emotional pain.

Denial is a stress response. It is quite normal to experience shock and denial when trauma or catastrophic loss occurs. The body's natural reaction to stress is to limit some functions so that other more essential functions take precedence. Some people experience this reaction as like being in a thick fog. They might know that others are with them, or that things are occurring around them, but the world seems hazy or obscure, and there is the sense of an emotional distance from everyone and everything. These people feel as if they are "going through the motions" in a state of unreality.

Others feel a heightened sense of awareness. They are on pins and needles, alert and ready for action. Emotionally keyed up, they vigilantly monitor noises, motions, and signs of threat. Whether lost in a fog or intensely alert, the sensations are disturbing. Some experience these sensations for only a short period, but others experience them for quite a while.

Grief can be disorienting. Men may feel confused, bewildered, or lost. Their sense of who they are has been assaulted; they're not accustomed to defining themselves as jobless, childless, single, or disabled. It's not unusual for men who have suffered a loss to describe themselves as strangers in a strange land or shepherds without sheep. Grieving gives them the sense of having lost all their moorings, and they grope desperately in search of something familiar and safe.

Denial is a normal human reaction to such disorientation. It helps men and women handle the stress and strain of everyday living by preserving or protecting their sense of self-worth. Denial does this by allowing us to ignore threatening, unpleasant, or unacceptable aspects of our external reality that seem to con-flict with our internal world. Simply put, defense mechanisms like denial let us maintain emotional stability by altering reality to fit our needs. In a sense, denial prevents us from coping rationally or directly with reality. The purpose of denial is to reorganize thoughts so that we feel less threatened. We then feel less anxious and fearful. Many of us welcome this relief, consciously or unconsciously.

For many of us, the anxiety caused by death or loss creates extreme physical and emotional tension. For a time, our lives are overshadowed by fears, and we seem to focus on little else. It is not just the unknown we fear; the known is even more hor-rifying. The reality of the loss is oppressive. Denial, then, becomes an important way to regulate emotional pain. Both men and women see this as a gain in short-term relief that aids their long-term adjustment. Denial is an active, not passive, attempt to cope with grief. It is the chance to shore-up reserves to address more confidently the challenge of grieving.

Grief dismantles our life. Slipping into denial helps us mini-mize this harsh reality. It also keeps us from dealing with our loss in a realistic fashion. While this may be necessary in the early days and weeks of our loss, sustained denial that keeps us from accepting the reality of a death or loss can be detrimental to our well-being. In its own way, denial silently sabotages the grieving process and prolongs it.

Men and women tend to view denial differently. From a woman's perspective, many men seem unwilling to face reality. When men fail to express their feelings or ask to be left alone to grieve, women see it as a quick prescription for trouble, and clear validation that the man is unfeeling and dispassionate.

Men are conditioned to control life. They feel that they must go on in the face of tragedy, appearing unemotional and content to carry their own burdens. This is what Larry Johnson tried to do. To be a man means you don't cry, you don't show weakness, you don't need support. Such an attitude can be slow poison, though, and some men know it. For others, however, the only real way to cope with grief is to resort to the same strategy they use in the rest of their emotional lives—denial.

Many men seem unwilling to face grief squarely in the eye. They feel they can best deal with the issue by avoiding it. They hope that grief will dissipate naturally with time. Keeping distracted and busy are well-practiced defenses, and many men expend considerable energy rejecting their current reality. It's easy to justify such behavior. Society expects men to be unemotional and to react less intensely to grief than women.

Men have learned from experience to push sensitive or painful issues out of their awareness. What is out of mind, is under control. To express their feelings would be humiliating— an admission of defeat. On the other hand, vigilantly repressing emotions is a Herculean task. The tension can become enormous, with few options for releasing that tension.

Many men both consciously and unconsciously restrict painful memories, thoughts, and emotions. They turn a key in a lock and walk away from everything on the other side of the door. They have not forgotten what happened; they have simply blocked it out of their conscious mind. Compartmentalizing their thoughts and emotions into tight little boxes creates emotional safety. By focusing on their job, repairing the car, getting on the Internet, or planning their team's next move on the basketball court, they keep threatening feelings and thoughts from overpowering them. Keeping active, busy, preoccupied is what's needed. It's not that death or loss has no effect. On the contrary, its effect is so great that men feel bound to reject reality and deny their emotions in order to cope with its aftermath. Denial is not an unwillingness to grieve, but a strategy for grieving. Men would have no reason to be in denial if their loss did not matter.

Cultivate confidence

When a man rejects his grief, it can feel to his partner as if he is rejecting her, too. She may assume that his absence of emtions for grieving is a sure-fire indicator that he may have no emotions for loving, either.

Seeing a partner in denial tends to exacerbate a woman's self-doubts and fears. A partner's inexpressiveness can be agonizing at a time when the woman wants and needs support and understanding. Feeling confident about surviving is hard when she feels so vulnerable and alone in her grief.

Difficult as it may be, a woman needs to slowly and deliberately cultivate confidence in herself, in her partner, and in their ability to survive together. Men use denial as self-defense, not as an attempt to discredit or nullify their relationship. Men have learned to police their feelings and keep their emotions to themselves. There is a double bind: suffer the consequences of being real with their feelings or do what they believe is expected of them.

No doubt, men pay a stiff price for denial, which worries most women. Keeping their feelings all on the inside is not something a woman would choose to do. Women know that stress compromises physical health. Women also worry that delaying grief will exacerbate it, causing more pain over time. Women have a right to be concerned, but getting enraged and overwrought is only going to increase anxiety and stress. Cultivating confidence may help women focus on those things they can control and feel good about.

Denial does seem selfish. It certainly is detrimental to intimacy and creates confusing messages in our relationships. It also can produce disturbing time warps that throw us out of sync with our partner. Truly, there are times when all of us would like to deny certain facts or events in our life. Yet denial as a place of retreat is much different than denial as a place of residence. Letting reality seep slowly into our consciousness can be a healthy way of coping.

5

Anger

You stole my imagination,
Burned in a stare. The memory of your back
Leaves a vacuum where I cannot touch you.
All hands reach for me with long fingernails,
Mocking consolation, making
My pupils boil black. Flames contort
In my emptiness, feeding on faces of sympathy,
Tempting me to look at myself.

—Louis Cerulli

The Wounded Animal Syndrome

When I was a teenager, I witnessed an accident in which a dog was hit by a car. I went over to help the injured animal and move him out of the street. The dog lashed out and bit me. He had been hurt and wanted to strike out at something. I just happened to be the closest thing to his anger.

There was a time when I felt just like that dog, crushed by life and waiting to bite the first hand that tried to help me. It all started one Saturday evening when my wife made a startling disclosure. In one breath she announced that dinner was ready and that she was leaving me. Within a half-hour she was gone. She refused to meet with me for any reason—to divide our possessions, break down the home, whatever. Ideally, I would have enjoyed lashing back at my ex-wife. I wanted to get even. I wanted her to hurt, and I felt entitled to my feelings.

We both worked at the same university, so it was inevitable that our paths would cross. The one day she stopped by my office, I took the opportunity to unload all the anger and frustration that had built up inside of me because of my grief. The situation turned ugly, and after she left, I felt shocked over my sudden display of rage and hostility.

The possibility of seeing her somewhere haunted me. We both traveled extensively for our work, and I became obsessed with the thought that I might accidentally run into her at the airport. I would walk into the terminal semiconsciously wondering if that woman over by the gate was her. I wasn't sure what I would do if I bumped into her, but part of me thought I might lose control and create another ugly scene.

I was infected with a deep anger, and it ruled my waking thoughts even when I was off doing something completely unrelated to my ex-wife. One Christmas my daughter and son-in-law invited me to his parents' farm in Virginia. The farm was a historic site, having been in their family for over three hundred years. The house was heated by a wood-burning furnace with timber from their own lot. The trees had to be cut down, then chopped into stove lengths. Unable simply to enjoy my time with my daughter, I directed my anger and rage toward the wood lot. The wood took the brunt of my feelings, and the pile grew substantially during my visit.

I feel it is all right to handle my grief by being angry, as long as I take it out in a way that is not harmful to anyone. At times, I am able to quell the wounded animal inside me, but I am never quite able to get rid of him. I can't seem to get past the feelings of vulnerability. Many evenings I stay up late feeling abandoned. I think that maybe it would have been different if I had left her, but she took the initiative, and now I'm left with the rejection.

Fourteen years after the divorce, I still have moments when I feel anger toward my ex-wife. I have not remarried and spend most of my time alone. I find it distressing to have no one with whom to share the day. When I feel the anger build in me, I try very hard not to take it out on my students, friends, or my children. It has been so long since my divorce, but sometimes the wound still feels raw.

—Robert W. Ross

Anger is considered one of the seven deadly sins. Anger displays itself in aggression, intimidation, and retaliation. Domestic violence, homicide, war, riots, gang rapes, and other aggressive acts find their roots in anger. Hostile work environments, dysfunctional lifestyles, and abusive relationships are also products of anger. Like a prison guard in the gun tower, anger controls and dominates the landscape it walks. There is no disputing that anger begets violence, destruction, and death. Anger is something most of us learn to fear.

Anger grows out of our insistence for satisfaction. From infancy, we want to direct life, to control it. A pin pricks, the bottle is too hot, the blanket is wrapped too tight, and the child wails in contempt. At the first sound of a baby's cries, parents rush to soothe and comfort. And so it goes with life. Attempts to restrain and to keep us from our desires, wants, and dreams cause us to rebel in self-defense. That state of rebellion often takes the form of anger.

Frustration is a powerful motivator. Most of us are unwilling to have our freedom threatened. We do not carelessly abandon our ideas, thoughts, or wants without a battle of some sort. We want what we want when we want it. Those who try to get in our way, challenge our beliefs, or thwart our goals must face our resistance. We respond reflexively. Sometimes our response is swift and explosive, other times it is slow and calculated. We may counter a threat with simple displeasure or a quick attempt to ignore or deflect the challenge. When repeatedly frustrated, we might erupt with resentment or even fury. Anger is a tightly knotted string of feelings that can intensify in force. Irritation, impatience, annoyance, resentment, rage, fury, and wrath are all part of the family of anger.

The origin of anger is not always easy to pinpoint. Injustice can ignite it; so can hurts, past and present. Most of us believe that we have rights, entitlements, privileges. When life obliterates these claims, we feel shocked and hurt. We see no justice in our child's death, our forced retirement, or the fragile state of our physical health. We know life isn't always fair, yet still we feel deprived, disillusioned, and angry. Injustice demands a response. Retribution is in order. We compel someone or something to pay for our pain. Anger becomes a means to an end.

We are all vulnerable to anger. Anger may be volatile, explosive, and destructive. The vengeance some seek in the name of anger can cause harm for generations. Yet anger also has a way of touching us and forcing us to stand up to the world. Anger says, "Pay attention to me, to my ideals and beliefs, to me as a person." Robert Ross's anger toward his wife had this element of wanting to be heard. At one time or another, all of us have, like Robert, felt slighted, ignored, or alienated. We may have worked hard to be the top-performing employee, the most attentive spouse, the best player on the golf course, and yet our accomplishments were discounted or overlooked.

When our self-image is challenged, we feel hurt and wounded. Anger is a way to assert ourselves and show our discomfort and dismay over how we are being treated. It can give us the strength and the resolve not to be ignored.

Anger is one of the few emotions society readily allows men to possess and to express. Anger is not only a sign of virility, it is the emblem of manhood. Society traditionally honors men's anger and authorizes it by providing men ample justification for its use. Men are given permission to be angry and, for the most part, are issued a license to display their anger without fear of recrimination. For men, anger is an entitlement that is both necessary and legitimate. An angry women is considered emotionally unstable and unfeminine, but an angry man is looked upon as having strength of character and moral conviction.

It comes as no surprise, then, to see men display anger, even rage, when they are grieving a loss. After all, loss gives us so much to be angry about. This is certainly how Robert felt. Grief is a terrible inequity. If a father's alcoholism leads to a heart attack or a career is ruined by a poor business decision, can we honestly say there is no justification for anger? Men expect life to go their way, and any challenge to that expectation is cause for anger. In fact, to react differently might seem suspicious, a cause for concern. Men have a duty to right life's wrongs.

Women are inclined to be angry in their grief, too. But the taboos and stereotypes against anger leave many women feeling unsupported and misunderstood. Their churning emotions may be interpreted as irritability and hostility. Fearing they will be ostracized, some women bury their anger and sink into depression. Some question their own worth and purpose for living, particularly when the loss is the death of a child.

For men, anger helps even the odds. Submitting to grief is admitting that you have lost control of your life, your family, and even yourself. Men are taught to stand up to challenges, using their anger as a shield or a weapon. Like the big bad wolf of nursery rhyme days, they huff and puff and try to blow grief away. Alas, grief is not so easily intimidated.

Grief threatens men. Its stranglehold endangers their sense of self, and they worry about exposing their true vulnerabilities. Like a wild pony running free in the high grasses, many men resist capture. They fear that their spirit will be broken and the true weight of their emotional pain will be displayed in plain view. Anger protects the male's core feelings. Anger that is big enough and strong enough helps defend his vulnerable inner self against exposure.

Men are taught that vulnerability equals weakness. To show any feeling other than anger is to risk being labeled a wimp. Few men want to be thought of as crybabies, yet many believe that this would be their fate should they venture out on life's bare limb and expose their emotions.

The truth is that men often lack the support they need to be comfortable with their emotions. As men, they have rarely placed themselves in situations where they could feel genuinely cared for. And without the external reference points that such support and care provides, there are few internal resources to draw on in times of need. Lacking support for their true feelings or validation of their loss, grieving men experience even minor frustrations as a major source of conflict. Like cars without shock absorbers, these men are jarred and damaged by every bump on the road. Gone is any tolerance for life's natural and commonplace irritations and disappointments. Without a cushion to soften the blow, anger replaces rationality and reasonableness.

When loss ensnares us in its sticky web, reality becomes chaotic. It is horrifying for a man to witness the stillbirth of his first-born child, to have a physician hand him a diagnosis of prostrate cancer, or to be told that a violent hurricane dragged his home off its foundation. Yet some men refuse to be pitied, and use anger to maintain an appearance of strength and independence. Anger eclipses their external reality and keeps others at arm's length, too afraid to offer support. It affects their internal reality, too, like a swift and effective anesthetic. With reality neutralized, men are oblivious to excruciating pain.

Men can feel a tremendous sense of guilt, regret, and even shame in grief. Society has bestowed on men the righteous honor of being protectors and defenders. The reality of grief leads many men to believe that they have somehow failed in what they sense as their most important life role. These feelings of degradation and self-loathing torture their soul, defying their sense of goodness and honor. Anger is a way to protest these emotions without slipping into an even deeper abyss of self-hatred. Anger is their protest against a past that is forever lost, a present that can never be restored, and a future that will never be.

Men and women both commonly direct their anger at specific people or circumstances they see as causing their personal tragedy. They experience a sense of being abandoned or let down by those who, they think, could have or should have prevented the disaster. Partners may blame each other for what has happened or feel angry about the way the other person is grieving. Blaming and finding fault are attempts to rationalize what we see as rejection (sometimes, in case of a death, even rejection by the loved one who has died) and to keep us from having to think of ourselves as bad, defective, or unlovable.

Men know there is energy and power in anger. When it races through them, they feel alive, empowered, forceful. The fact that anger demands attention helps some regain a bit of control over their otherwise uncontrollable lives. They feel as if they are actively doing something, not just waiting to be ambushed by grief. Anger is not passive. It reassures men that they are not helpless, that they can make progress and perhaps even move ahead in their grieving.

Men can easily abuse the energy and power of anger. Men know that if sufficiently threatened, anger can be their greatest survival tool, the big stick capable of beating their enemy into submission. For some men, the threat grief poses to their sense of self is sufficient to cause them to strike out. Anger becomes all-consuming and turns into rage, damning and destroying everything and everyone in its path. Such men become predators, acting out with physical violence, abusiveness, and intimidation. Ironically, their lives spin even further out of control, and they are no closer to a resolution of their loss.

It is apparent that some men rely heavily on anger when they grieve. Anger works for men. It protects, it camouflages, and it gives men a dose of control. Anger is a start at healing, a mechanism for coping and externally releasing some of what is brewing inside. It may be the only recognizable tool in some men's toolbox. Whether a man's use of anger is healthy and realistic is an individual issue. Troubling and cruel as it can be, anger is a bonafide emotion and confirmation that men are feeling *something*.

Respond, don't react

Rather than reacting to anger, women need to respond to it. A man's anger pushes his partner away. Quite naturally, she fears his wrath and over time can be worn down emotionally, mentally, and even spiritually. His anger convinces her that he is unsympathetic and dispassionate about their loss and most certainly about her feelings. When a woman reacts with insults, accusations, or lengthy diatribes of past indignities, she only pours salt on already raw, open wounds. Crying buckets of tears, slamming doors, or employing "the silent treatment" will not heal any wounds, either.

Very little good comes from reacting to anger. Rarely is anger rational. Instead, women need to respond to anger, addressing it head-on. Knowing that hurt, frustration, and insecurity lie underneath anger gives women the strength to stand up to it. Anger rarely expresses itself as a single emotion. It is more often a charlatan, and women must learn not to accept her mate's outbursts, tirades, or hostile disposition at face value.

Since the time of cavemen, men have used anger to fend off the enemy. Men sometimes frame life in terms of simple conflicts: predator or prey, survival or death. Today's enemy is grief—and the threat it poses to the man's emotional vulnerabilities. Women who push on these vulnerabilities unknowingly become the enemy target. Reacting to anger only reinforces it.

Women are not the enemy. Neither are they responsible for controlling their partner's anger or for stabilizing his emotions. An important basic rule in lifeguard training is to stay afloat without being pulled under. Women need to deflect anger with firmness and care. Setting clear limits and boundaries will help keep women from being consumed or controlled by their partner's anger. Women must own their feelings and attempt to maintain emotional stability.

6

Control

When the sky's stomach swelled,
You wound around my leg, tiny handfuls
Of corduroy. My veins, woven steel,
Mortar in my joints, I surrounded you
And you counted the space between thunderclaps.
Now, your fingers scarred from climbing
Out of my stronghold, you erect a fortress
Without an entrance.

—Louis Cerulli

A Grief Resolved

In the busy flow of a large dental practice, marriage, and a family of four children, there were few times to pause and to evaluate the direction of my life. Everything seemed under control, until my son, Jay, ran away. He was sixteen and into addictive drugs. Jay and I were both strong willed, and we argued constantly. Gwen, my wife, was in the middle, like an innocent civilian in a war. As the dominant parent, I made it clear that I would not tolerate drugs in my home. After several months of tiresome conflict, Jay found that it was easiest to abandon ship. One spring day, he packed up his rebuilt VW and took off for parts unknown.

The feelings of separation and abandonment were devastating. My pride and reputation had been struck. I asked myself, "Why had Jay left us? Where had I failed as a parent? When did we stop talking and start arguing?" I felt as if I had no control over Jay or the situation. I began desperately searching for answers.

I found it difficult to believe that I could have done something wrong in raising Jay. Up until he ran away, I felt that I lived a good life and made the right decisions for my family. I had established a successful business and marriage. I provided for my family the way I was taught to. I was involved with the church, performing community services and donating time. Jay's leaving made me feel unsuccessful; it was almost as if he had taken my public image with him when he left.

I began to feel tremendous grief and guilt over Jay's disappearance from my life. My experience of loss was like a winding road with shifting landscapes. Traveling this route, each turn provided some agonizing phase of pain and remorse. I kept returning to fruitless tasks. On every street, with every passing vehicle, I searched for a blue van with a red-haired driver. Often, I made illegal U-turns to chase what appeared to be my son.

When I couldn't find the answers within, I turned to books for answers to my problems. I sought hidden secrets of parenting through child psychology and often read well into the night. Of the hundreds of pages I read, I couldn't find any clear answers to my problems with Jay.

Turning to close friends, I received sympathy but no real answers. "Boys are like that," they said, or "It'll all turn out okay." Another friend remarked, "Yes, we're having a tough time with our daughter, too, but she'll straighten out. Your boy will, too." Sometimes, when I ran into friends accidentally, they seemed embarrassed to talk about Jay. It was difficult seeing them struggle with whether or not to bring up "the subject."

Next, I turned to psychiatry, and it was onto "the couch." I reviewed the events of my early life—my struggles, conflicts, victories, and losses. Of all the things I learned in counseling, my resolution to reduce my dental practice and spend more quality time with Gwen and our children seemed the most productive. Still, I felt unable to solve my problems with Jay. The direction I sought to alleviate my feelings of failure was not found in counseling.

Still confused, I turned to the church for answers. I wanted to confide in our friends among the clergy. After many long talks and prayers, I still wondered where God fit into all of my dilemmas. Once again, I received sympathy and assurances, but no real answers.

Just as everything seemed hopeless, I found what I needed in an unusual place. A group of nearly twenty people came to our church to lead a weekend retreat. Men and women from varied backgrounds shared their spiritual transformations with us. There was a youth group as well, but they met separately. I was not

*especially excited about this evangelistic event. I wanted no part
in a "sawdust trail" sort of thing, but a distinguished professor of
dentistry and his wife were part of the group of visiting
evangelists. The hospitality chairman asked if Gwen and I would
host the couple, and we agreed. We were encouraged by their
warmth and down-to-earth manner and considered giving the
retreat a try.*

*We listened to people recount their experiences, errors, and
struggles. I felt an affinity with their hardships and slowly warmed
up to the spirituality they presented. When the retreat came to a
close on Sunday morning, the church service opened with some
great hymns of faith. These were songs that I had heard and sung
for most of my life. Somehow they took on a new meaning.*

*Then came a moment that I dreaded. Whatever happened, I
had resolved never to respond to an "altar-call," which might
require an emotional outburst. But the evangelist made a novel
suggestion. He invited everyone to use slips of paper provided in
the pews to write something they wanted to give to God. We
were to place these slips into a cardboard box in front of the
altar and then return to our seats. This seemed unobtrusive, and
I decided to participate.*

*I surprised myself by what I wrote on the paper, "God, I give
you my son, Jay, and each of our children, for I simply don't know
what to do for them." Having recognized my utter inability to fix
everything that had gone wrong, I asked God for help. Instead of
feeling relieved, I felt emotionally smashed! My knees buckled. I
could not rise. All the anger, frustration, and sorrow of the past
months flooded me like a deluge.*

*After a few moments, I felt arms behind me lifting me to my
feet. Turning, there was Jay, my runaway boy. He said, "Dad, I just
gave my drugs to God." I replied, "Jay, I just gave you to God." We*

hugged for the first time in months, and I finally felt a connection with my son. In struggling so hard to hold on to my family, I had lost everything of importance. When I finally relinquished control of Jay, God gave him back to me.

—J. B. Blair

Freedom is an important value in our society. Debated almost daily in political circles, universities, at the job, and on the subway platform, the idea of freedom assumes that people can function as independent, autonomous beings. To be labeled independent is a source of pride, as it implies a strong, capable person. Dependence, on the other hand, is a fairly negative attribute that suggests a weak or inferior person. There are certain rights, responsibilities, and privileges that we normally associate with freedom and independence. One is power. The more of it we have, the freer we feel. Whether for good or bad, power lets us create, act, and do. Most of us prefer to have power over our decisions, actions, and choices rather than allow others to manipulate or control our life. External control is a toxic concept in our culture of self-reliance.

Most of us believe that the freedom to make decisions and choose options gives us control of life and, consequently, of our future. We tend to react pretty strongly when we feel that our autonomy is threatened, particularly when the threat comes from forces outside of us. Such threats are often seen as intentional and malicious. We react against the pressure to change and out of a need to protect ourselves and those things we value.

Limits or challenges to our independence disturb us, make us feel uncomfortable and uneasy. Some of us may feel hostile and aggressive toward the people or things that threaten us. Many times we want someone to make amends for what has happened. Quite often threats cause us to reprioritize our thinking, and we become more self-directed. Resisting the threat reinforces the sense that we are in charge. We determine that we can do what we want; we resist doing those things we don't want to do.

A personal tragedy throws our life into a tailspin. Like J.B. Blair, our self-image and self-concept can be challenged in significant ways. Where we once comfortably believed that we controlled our own destiny, we may now feel helpless, powerless, and defeated. We may blame ourselves for the fatal car accident that killed our parent or for the onset of a malignant melanoma in our child. We imagine that we could have prevented the tragedy, and we judge ourselves a failure.

Most of us consider ourselves loving, considerate, and fair-minded. The idea that we are somehow to blame for our loss is shocking and frightening. Our integrity, honor, and values are at stake. If we're not to blame, then some outside force or element is. The world, then, is unjust and cruel. Our tragedy results either from random events beyond our control or from our own poor judgment and inadequacies. Neither conclusion is reassuring. We have failed to control either our environment or our own life. Perhaps that is what J.B. initially thought, too.

In our culture, men are expected to be in control, in all situations and at all times, whether at home, work, or in a social environment. Men must not show weaknesses of any kind, or be overly dependent on others for support, advice, or encouragement. They are encouraged to be dominant, aggressive, powerful and capable. If men don't have the answer, they're supposed to know where and how to find it.

Most men approach life believing that there isn't a problem that can't be solved. They know that if they were to think about it, fiddle with it, tinker here or there with it, put some muscle into it, or read an instruction manual about it, they would be bound to find a solution and fix it. For many men, grief is just another problem to solve—just another of life's challenges, another test of manhood.

Every man knows that manhood is about challenge and achievement. One must win the competition and walk away with the trophy, whether that trophy be a wife, a job, a golf game, a house, a low cholesterol level, large biceps, or a big bank account. These achievements don't come from teamwork; they come from personal effort and self-reliance. Success comes by one's own hands and by one's own means. To achieve success in any other way might indicate a lack of ability or courage.

Though women are neither dependent nor helpless, many don't seem to have the same problem-solving drive or need to prove themselves that men have. Generally speaking, women are more flexible about how they face problems, even though they want things to go smoothly and sometimes can be quite demanding in their desire to remedy problems. Some things do feel insolvable to women. Grief can be one of those things.

Women don't necessarily see themselves as lone wolves. Grief is an intensely personal challenge, yet it also is a relational challenge. Women want to be comforted and understood. Most want others to grieve with them, working cooperatively to process feelings, hurts, and disappointments. Their need for intimacy and emotional ties makes women uncomfortable grieving in solitude. Grief is not something women want to resolve entirely on their own.

Being a man is about being brave. Men learn early in life that they should try to tolerate physical and emotional pain without flinching. They're taught that suffering is a badge of honor: "no pain, no gain." Men cannot afford to lose face by having others see them as cowardly, timid, or faint-hearted. To be brave demonstrates a strong character and personal resolve. We hold in esteem men who are called courageous, daring, valiant, heroic. These traits are what men aspire to. To be less than brave is to be less than a man.

Women take pride in being considered brave, yet they are less likely than men to emphasize overt displays of physical bravery or measure their worth by the amount of pain they can endure. Women know they can be brave, resilient, gutsy in ways different from men. They don't necessarily care to demonstrate or prove their bravery. Most women exhibit enormous bravery in their grieving. Going through labor with a baby that has died in utero or watching a parent slowly move from independence to complete dependence takes a special kind of strength. Yet there are limits to how brave women feel they need to be. Unlike men, being brave doesn't make a woman any more of a woman.

When life abruptly goes out of control, one feels powerless. Men react negatively to this sense of powerlessness; they resist playing the role of the helpless victim. They want to make life safe and predictable again, for themselves and for those around them. Not only do many men feel that they must stop grief from causing further damage, they also feel that they should make someone or something pay for the destruction that has already been caused. Exerting control is something men feel that they *can* do, and do well.

Traditionally, the man is expected to protect and provide for his family. If he or his family has been harmed by grief, he may feel that he has failed to fulfill this traditional role. Ashamed, some men assume the role of manager and attempt to make up for their failure by diligently trying to fix everyone in their family. They listen, support, comfort, and empathize, pushing their own pain to the background to accomplish the task at hand. If they can get everything in their family under control, they believe, then they can restore harmony and reestablish their role as family guardian. If it were possible, they would willingly transfer all their family's pain, heartache, and suffering onto themselves.

Women want to know that they can depend on their partner for support. When confronted with tragedy, many women yearn for a stable and responsible "father figure." This need for a father figure may demand a level of intimacy and involvement that men are not be used to and can create even more anxiety and discomfort.

Grieving men sometimes look for ways to escape the home. It's not that the home is a battleground, but rather that it holds too many depressing reminders of what has been lost. For some men, it has ceased to be the showcase of competence, the place of pride and honor thatit once was. Late nights at the office, frequent trips across town on errands, and excuses to eat dinner out are attempts to legitimize the male's avoidance of the home and, indirectly, to reassert control. As the sense of dread continues to fester, some men compulsively seek out evening and weekend activities that will keep them a safe distance from home which has lost its appeal as a comfortable and reassuring place.

Men are competitive beings. Inundated with images of superhuman masculinity in mass culture, they like to imagine themselves as "Men of Steel." Physical strength is traditionally a defining male trait. In many men's minds, no one or no thing should be able to defeat the well-prepared male, and so they react to grief by preparing themselves for battle. Some grieving men become obsessed with their physical health, others with their mental health. Diet, exercise, stress management, meditation, and spiritualism may all become part of the man's new regimen. Women are sometimes surprised when the dinner table conversation suddenly turns from the usual discussion about who didn't put the lawn mower away to talk of the virtues of cholesterol-free eggs.

Much more so than women, men define themselves by the kind of work they do. Work affirms masculinity; men feel competent, responsible, self-reliant while at work. Working harder and longer than others is a tried-and-true way to solve problems and garner rewards. Grieving men know that their moral strength and character will be affirmed if they can appear strong and unfazed before their coworkers. The admiration of coworkers ensures status and respect, things that grief tries to wipe out. More than just a place of escape, men see that the job can also be a safe and legitimate place to work out aggression and anger about the world and its unjustness.

Leisure activities can take on a new importance when men grieve. Men may immerse themselves in countless things—from sexual behavior, to competitive sports, to reorganizing the fishing tackle box. They may involve themselves in hobbies, or join civic groups and professional organizations, but what they choose to do usually isn't as important to them as the mere act of doing something, and doing it well. Activities organize, structure, and concentrate men's time and thoughts. They are an effective way to occupy time and, in the process, distract men from their grief and pain. If their feet don't stop moving, men sometimes believe, maybe nothing bad can catch them.

Many men resist the notion that the world is a random and volatile place. They believe that they can and must stop the injustice their tragedy has placed on their family before it affects other unsuspecting victims. Their tragedy must stand for something. To create meaning from their loss, many men devote great amounts of time and energy to issues or concerns related to their personal tragedy. They may, for example, mobilize groups to fight teen suicide, educate the public about the effects of depression, lobby government entities against the tobacco industry, volunteer in hospice programs, organize AIDS marathons, develop programs for bereaved families, or lead cancer support groups.

Sometimes, the activities grieving men seek out can be harmful to themselves or their family. Some men may drink heavily, use drugs, or indulge themselves in a sexually promiscuous manner. Others may push the limits of their physical strength in risk-taking ventures. Still others may get into serious physical altercations, or take on job assignments that put their life in danger. A grieving man's sense of vulnerability and fear of rejection can be so powerful that he feels he has no choice but to do things that prove he is invincible and fearless. Grieving women, too, take unnecessary risks, like foregoing a seat belt, driving excessively over the speed limit, or relying on prescription drugs or alcohol. Grief is an invitation to self-destruction for both sexes.

Some men perceive grief as a test of their manhood. Not wanting to be labeled weak or powerless, they set out to prove they are brave, competent, and self-sufficient—in other words, "real men." Some challenge themselves in daring and dangerous ways; others immerse themselves in countless activities and responsibilities. All men want to find a way to ensure that bad things will stop happening to them and to those they love and care about. By getting their life under control, they believe they've bought the best insurance policy available.

Practice reasonable tolerance

It is very hard to be on the receiving end when your partner is controlling or manipulative, especially when his behaviors are obsessive or potentially self-destructive. His frenetic pace may feel less like he's trying to fix things and more like he's trying to avoid things. You may have a difficult time getting a real sense of his feelings of helplessness and fear of abandonment when publicly he acts competent, unemotional, charged, and ready for battle. It certainly is confusing to hear him tell friends and coworkers that everything is fine when the family is close to collapsing. This is the time for women to practice reasonable tolerance, empathizing with the unrealistic and unhealthy cultural expectations placed on men, yet keeping to limits and boundaries that maintain her worth and value as a person.

Women may interpret their partner's controlling behaviors as a lack of love and care. Poor communication is common when we already feel wounded and vulnerable. Communicating is especially difficult when what each of us wants is to be built up emotionally, not taken apart even more. By practicing reasonable tolerance, women are mindful of what they want and need from their partner, as well as what they don't want and need. Women need not be passive or subordinate their needs. Each partner has a right to hold the other accountable for those actions and behaviors that compromise their intimacy.

No matter how hard your partner tries, he can't fix you or completely repair the tragedy that has affected your family. By the same token, you can't fix him. The shame, guilt, anxiety, and irritability he feels is something that you cannot completely mollify, nor should you try. Whether rational or irrational, his motivations come from his innermost need to make his world safe and secure again. As intimate partners, you have mutual desires, dreams, and hopes. To love well and to survive together takes a joint effort.

7
Bitterness

Your breath smells like decaying leaves.
Your teeth, dyed with Autumn's paint, are
Framed by a perpetual sneer. I'm afraid
To see my face outlined in your cheekbones.
I try not to walk with your sideways lean.
I lay dreams on your plate and you feed
Me sand. I've swallowed a desert,
Embittered by a flickering form.

—Louis Cerulli

Fatherless

For the majority of my life, my father was absent. Though I could feel his presence physically, there was never any emotional guidance, intimacy, or connection between us. Now I am in my late thirties and, with all the time I've spent around my father, I don't really know him. Our relationship worked backwards; the more time I spent with him, the less I really knew him. I felt frustrated that he didn't know me, either, even though I tried repeatedly to show him who I was. After resigning myself to the fact that the relationship would be tenuous at best, I told my father to leave my life.

It wasn't an easy decision to make, because in some ways I respected my father. He had a strong work ethic that I wanted to emulate. Unfortunately, he took work to such an extreme that it was all he cared about. I found it difficult to be around him because he used work as a way to measure my worth. Any value I had was based on the work I performed, the profession I entered, or my success in life.

As a young child, I saw my friends and their fathers do all the normal things that dads and sons do, like playing ball or going to sporting events. My dad never fulfilled those kinds of expectations for me. I felt as if some part of myself, some key relationship, was missing. I desperately wanted my father to teach me something fruitful or beneficial about being male. On the outside I was normal, but inside, where memories of my dad should have been, there was a muted space. It was like having some disfiguration that only I could see.

As I grew up, it became more and more important to me to be accepted and acknowledged by my father. Just once, I wanted him to tell me that he was proud of me for something, anything. I suspect that he may have told others he was proud of me, but I was never privy to that information. I saw him as harsh, apa-thetic, and uncaring.

I remember my senior year in high school. I had no clue where I would go when I finished my studies. I wondered what I would do and what I was really all about. I went to my dad for direction and support in helping me choose between college or trade school. It was my hope that we could work together to decide my ultimate profession, but my father responded ineffectually, saying I should find something I was good at and just do that for the rest of my life. The advice felt worthless because I didn't know what I liked to do or what I was good at.

Though I felt frustrated and shamed, I went to him a second time and asked for his help with a number of tasks, like filling out financial aid forms and meeting with college reps. Once again my father offered me an empty plate. He said that he wasn't inter-ested in helping me or assisting me financially, but he did say that I had better figure out what I was going to do and do it, then move out.

Not long after that incident, I came home from school with exciting news. My English teacher had written me a terrific rec-ommendation for college. As I walked up the driveway, I found a brand new car and van sitting in front of the garage. I couldn't imagine where these had come from because my father had made it perfectly clear that he didn't have the money to help me with college. I felt outraged. After expressing my frustration, my father responded coldly, saying that the vehicles made my mother and him happy and so I should be happy. Oh really, I thought. My father's shaming words made me angry and resent-ful. Like so many other times in my life, I was expected to ignore my own feelings and to focus on my father.

To this day, my father has continued to put himself first and remain ignorant of my needs. He believes that satisfaction is found in having a new car, clean clothes, and a full refrigerator. He gives no thought to love, relationships, or tenderness. My father glossed over the simple gestures in life, like teaching me to fish or to fly a kite. Instead, I was left with the stern message that I was to do it right the first time, but I had no understanding as to what the right way was.

The breaking point in our relationship occurred when my mother was hospitalized. I had chosen to grieve over her deteriorating health at home. I wanted to be alone because I didn't want to risk an argument with my father in front of her. My father telephoned, and for an instant I thought he was going to ask me how I was dealing with everything, but he immediately began to criticize my decision not to come to the hospital. After all those years of emotional estrangement, he still couldn't understand how I wasn't able to take his judgments and fault-finding. I made it clear that my absence was not about my mother, but about him. After nearly thirty years of disappointment and anger, I found it impossible to control my feelings about my father. In a torrent of emotion, I told my father to get out of my life, finally letting go of all my bitterness and resentment.

Since that day, there have been many times that I have longed for a father. Now that I have my own child, I am thankful that I am able to meet her needs, given the incomplete blueprint of fatherhood that was drawn for me. With her help, I am defining what a father should be, but I still resent the thought of her growing up without a grandfather. I had always expected that my dad would fit some kind of mold, but reality has painted quite another picture.

—John L. Jankord

Much of how we react to life is based on our expectations. The thought that life is fair, that good things happen to good people, that hard work will be rewarded, all come from a sense of confidence about how life is. Our expectations about the world are grounded in our past experiences, and help us predict present-day reality. We expect our mail to be delivered every day at 2:00 PM, the morning newspaper to be lying on our front steps when we wake, and the garbage truck to show up on Wednesdays. We depend on these things to occur, because they always occur. The mail, the newspaper, the garbage pickup are part of the rhythms and movements in our life, and we know they are certain to take place again and again.

Most of the time we expect reality to be predictable, equitable, and relatively unambiguous. Such expectations make us feel more secure, diminish our fears, and increase our sense of satisfaction, emotionally and interpersonally. When we anticipate that things will go our way, there is an accompanying feeling of control. Life feels manageable. The confidence we gain gives us strength for the normal ups and downs of life.

Expectations set our life course and support our dreams. We use them to guide our decision making and direct our behavior. Expectations can influence how we react to others and how they react to us. Some of us may find ourselves drawn to a weeping woman we happen upon at the cemetery; others may turn away, afraid or embarrassed to intrude. In either case, our reaction is based on our assumptions about the woman and our own private expectations about our behavior, attitude, and motivations. We expect ourselves to be as predictable as we hope others will be.

The expectation that life will be orderly is a wonderful ideal, but sooner or later we all come to realize that there are no guarantees in life. The routines that structured our life can vanish overnight. The parent we loved so deeply can die, the job and its prospects for a successful life can end, the business we built day by day can collapse in ruin. Through personal tragedy we learn a disturbing and painful lesson: though life is often predictable, sometimes it is extremely unpredictable. Randomness, disorder, and chaos do exist in our world.

Accepting the fact that life is uncontrollable is not an easy task for either gender. Generally speaking, women trust in their ability to persevere, but many look to their primary relationships for protection and security. When that security is shattered by death, loss, or personal tragedy, women can become disillusioned and resentful. The perception that their partner has abandoned them or let them down can be crushing and debilitating. The rejection, shame, and disappointment women feel can fester into a gnawing sense of bitterness. Women may then find fault with their partner, becoming spiteful or vindictive.

When life doesn't go their way, men tend to feel powerless and angry. Like John Jankord, they sense rejection and brood about what has been lost. Men want to be victorious in life, and the thought that they have failed is devastating. These feelings are compounded by the fear that life will never get better. Filled with self-doubt, some men rely on sarcasm to lessen their disappointment. Their caustic attitude reflects disillusionment with life and the bitter feelings they hold inside.

Bitterness is an elusive emotion. It is more than just anger; it is fermented anger. Bitterness is expressed as sarcasm, resignation, and resentment. Men show bitterness when they blame themselves or others for their tragedy, or when they feel frustrated and hopeless about life. Bitterness is about feeling ashamed. The souring of emotions that constitutes bitterness fosters loneliness and leads to despair.

The reality of a death or loss makes some men feel that life has betrayed them. They know that they have made many sacrifices in pursuit of the good life. When grief invalidates these sacrifices, they feel angry and disgusted. The unfairness is intolerable. They know they deserve more from life, and they feel they have been sabotaged and shamed. The world no longer seems fair or just, and they become hopeless about their life and their ability to succeed and be happy. Outraged, such men turn the pain inward and let bitterness fester and brew.

Many women feel bitterness, too. Life has disappointed them. They have been victimized unfairly. They lament over why the death or loss occurred, and they wonder if they might have brought it all upon themselves. Comparing their life to others, women often think they have been singled out for disaster.

Some men respond to disappointment by lashing out and placing the blame for what has happened on the actions and behaviors of others—an unreasonable boss, an idiotic driver, an irresponsible partner. Other men may blame themselves, rationalizing that if only they would have been more attentive, worked more hours, or tried harder, their relationship would still be intact, their job would be secure, the accident would not have occurred. Blaming others is a way for men to defend themselves and justify their actions, while self-blaming is a way to punish themselves in the hope that the world won't punish them further. By punishing themselves, men stay in control of their emotional pain and ward off further rejection. Yet blame doesn't provide relief from the deep hurt, discouragement, and anger that many men feel.

Men believe that they are capable of doing grand things and that they will make a difference in the world. Being served with divorce papers or being told of an inoperable tumor isn't what they had in mind. Neither do men want to feel that they couldn't protect their families from harm, that they weren't the war hero they imagined, or that they were unable to ease a wife's grief. The clash of expectations and reality shakes their self-respect and self-identity.

This loss of self can make men feel shameful. Their sense of being acceptable, lovable, and worthwhile is severely threatened. Grief has pointed out their failures and deficiency, and men feel shamed in response. Worried about their self-respect, men cover up their feelings of inadequacy and defectiveness by rationalizing and denying their pain. Even with these tactics, men can't help but judge themselves a failure and believe that life has neglected them, too. The end result is bitterness and resentment for what they failed to do.

Society's standards reinforce men's sense of failure. Society expects men to be stoic in their grief, and those men who dare express their feelings are certain to be ridiculed. Mourning publicly is all too risky for most men because of their worries about the punishment they will endure. For many men, acting like a man has never been so hard as when they are in the midst of tragedy.

Men can feel shame when they sense that they are not living up to their partner's standards of good grieving. Many women accuse their partners of being in denial about emotional pain and avoiding the work of processing grief. Women get discouraged and angered by men's silence and unwillingness to discuss feelings openly. Women's interpretation that men are insensitive and uncaring often turns to criticism and shaming remarks. These words and accusations make men feel defective and painfully self-conscious. Caught in the dilemma of maintaining their masculinity while trying to respect their partner's needs, many men begin to feel embittered about the conflicting roles and expectations in their life.

Men resent grief for trying to wrong and injure them. They feel insulted by the pain and suffering forced upon their life. Death or loss isn't part of their plan, and it certainly isn't something they anticipated. Though men feel prepared to handle any adversity, they are indignant about the extreme emotional distress that accompanies grief. The unfairness is incomprehensible. They are unwilling to witness the pain of their own humanity. For many men, resentment becomes a point of impasse as they are reluctant to admit that they may not be as all-powerful and in control as they once felt.

Part of feeling powerful for men is the belief that they make good decisions and are competent people. Yet when their life is changed by personal tragedy, men wonder what they did wrong or why they are being punished so severely. Most men are filled with questions about why this happened to them and not to some other nameless, faceless person. They feel offended by the thought that perhaps they were an innocent victim.

Men reject the notion of being a victim. Bad things might happen to them, but men believe there is always a reason for these actions. They want to know what rule they broke or how they fell out of favor with the world. For men, there must be a rational explanation why all this has happened. Without that reason, a sense of hate and bitterness begins to develop.

Looking for an answer to why life did not work out is trying for men. There are so many questions, so few logical answers. After all the effort of wearing out their whys, men often come face to face with regret. The past, present, and future can seem like a lopsided house of cards, an impossible structure with little hope of repair. If only they could change what was or restore tomorrow, then their life would not feel so broken. The regret for all the things they could have, should have, or would have done differently is a burning sorrow.

Men feel bitterness over their wasted time and forfeited wishes. It hurts greatly to know that what they once believed in will never come true. For many, time is merely a daily reminder of all the things gone wrong. The indignation and shame defrauds men of hope. Believing their situation is futile, they succumb to bitterness and resentment. Their poisonous attitude is filled with sarcasm, contempt, scorn, mockery. The rancor they feel is an attempt to reject grief and all its devastation. Like denial, the solitude that bitterness can provide keeps men's emotional pain at a safe distance. Men must avoid grief and disappointment, and bitter feelings are a way to push away from the hurt.

Pursue compassion

Men feel bitter and resentful when they are concerned and frustrated about their place in the world and their ability to fulfill their responsibilities. Blaming and shaming others and themselves, they become discouraged and feel condemned to failure. This sense of not living up to one's own standards or not gaining approval can slowly wither their soul. Longing for some relief from the clenching grip of their bitterness, men struggle to have hope. For women, the harsh change in their partner's attitudes is unsettling and can aggravate their own disturbing emotions.

Women need to pursue compassion to heal their brokenness. The sadness and loneliness we feel is real. Our partner's bitterness feels like rejection, and we question their love and bond of intimacy. We expected our partner to experience the loss in the same way and at the same time. It is alarming to know that this is far from true.

It is unlikely that you will grieve identically to your partner or that your loss will have the same degree of meaning. Grief is too complex and personal. The emotions, behaviors, and attitudes of your partner may feel so dissimilar as to be distressing. Personalizing these differences, you may think it's all about you. This may be especially true with bitterness and resentment. Just because you witness or are the target of your partner's bitterness does not mean that you are the source of that bitterness. Only when you can separate from his actions will you be free to pursue compassion for yourself and for him.

Bitterness creates a lingering state of emotions. Hurtful as these feelings are, they give us cause to examine the direction our life is going and to decide what really matters. Grief presents many possibilities for us and our path to intimacy. The threats posed by bitterness prompt us to keep our heart open, willing to heal and change. This period of soul-searching is a time to treat ourselves with kindness and to let ourselves be influenced by that kindness. In so doing, we will be able to show kindness to our partner and spark a change in them as well. Life can get better. Contemplating changes in our attitudes and doing something to make life better are up to us. To alter the course of bitterness takes determination and compassion.

8

Addictive Behaviors

I inject delusion in steady doses,
Drowning in my own skin.
Jumbled faces of failure
Trace my mistakes across the water in
Ever-widening circles. I'm half-asleep
In coral reefs, scraping my wrists on their
Horns. Silence flickers beneath my
Eyes and days mimic years.

—Louis Cerulli

The Price of Success

At age thirty, I accepted a position as Senior Psychologist in a large county mental health center. My advancement to the position had seemed to happen logically, the final step in a long series of successful endeavors. I had graduated from college with a Ph.D., married, and started a wonderful family. Each time I had changed jobs, I had furthered my knowledge, gradually honing my skills for that one ideal job. When the opportunity to head a day treatment center presented itself, I thought that fate had thrown yet another reward in my lap. The position appeared well suited to my interests, abilities, and goals. My duties involved directing the center for outpatient psychiatric clients and consulting with numerous community agencies. In addition, I carried a caseload of individual psychotherapy clients.

The job was extremely stimulating, and quite a coup for such a young man. I funneled all of my creativity and ambition into turning the day treatment center into a model program. Community agencies widely accepted us, and my reputation as a consultant flourished. I felt like the expert and wore the badge with pride. I derived meaning from the knowledge that I was helping others. My energy level was high, and the positives in my work spilled over to enhance my family life.

Nevertheless, a black cloud loomed over my numerous achievements. The chief psychiatrist of the hospital that housed our day treatment center caused much of my grief. He had many undesirable traits, but his alcoholism was the worst. He was threatened by the day treatment center's success, which in large part reflected my contribution. He continually made attempts to disband the center and cut off my access to consulting activities.

The chief psychiatrist attempted to sabotage the success of the day treatment center. I found him to be dishonest, power-hungry, and insecure. He was envious of the loyalty that other professionals and agencies in the community showed me. He made it clear that he would tolerate no rivals to his power.

After two years as Senior Psychologist, I had developed a pervasive sense of doom. My growing fear was that I would be dismissed from my job. One evening I received a telephone call informing me that my job had been terminated. I was given no opportunity to transfer cases and general responsibilities to other professionals.

Initially, I coped with my dismissal by becoming an over-achiever. I began to work an inordinate number of hours in an effort to feel good about myself again. My health and relationships started to deteriorate, and I spent more and more time focused on work. I wanted to ensure I would never feel professionally insecure again. When I was putting in seventy to eighty hours a week at work, I didn't have time to think about how bad everything had turned out. My work increasingly became the focus of my life. I used it as a channel to mask all of my insecurities and fears. I made sure that my actions were so ethical that no one could criticize me ever again. I struggled to improve myself in every action that I performed. My perfectionism affected my family life, and there were times when they wondered where my compulsive behaviors would end.

Many evenings, I would think about how I reacted and what I learned from being fired. I even thought sometimes that my negative experiences with the day treatment center accurately reflected my abilities and contributions as a person. I questioned if the dismissal could have been justified. As I grieved over the loss of such a perfect job, I wondered if I would ever have such an opportunity again. I felt as if I had failed at my one chance to do something important. Now, I was left to face obscurity. These thoughts had a severe impact on my self-worth, and I often went to bed feeling frustrated and hopeless.

I finally reached a crisis at age forty. My workaholic behavior spiraled out of control and brought me to the point of total burnout. I wondered if I wanted to continue my career as a psychologist at all.

Eventually, I followed the advice I had taught other workaholic men in therapy. I limited my workweek to forty hours and forced myself to develop other personal interests, including spending more time with my wife and kids. I also developed an extensive number of friendships. These involvements created new priorities in my life and kept me from returning to my dysfunctional work patterns.

It took me many years to see the positives in my life after the dismissal. The long-term impact on my professional and personal life was profound, and my career had more of an effect on my well-being than any other area of my life. I encountered more stress, grief, and difficult emotions from my job than with my family and other personal relationships. While I ultimately developed many strategies that were helpful with work and life in general, I am still feeling the effects of the past.

—Richard Friberg

At one time or another all of us have felt physical pain.
Perhaps the pain was from something as minor as a cut on the
finger when a sharp knife slipped from your grasp while slicing
an apple. Possibly it was caused by something more serious,
like a tumble down a flight of stairs that sent you to the emer-
gency room with a punctured lung and broken ribs. The sensation of physical pain alerts us that our body has been trauma-
tized. Typical reactions to physical pain may be a sudden tear-
ful outburst, a rush of anxiety, or a sense of fear or panic.
Some people resort to a barrage of obscenities or ridicule themselves for their apparent imprudent or inappropriate behavior.
Physical pain is uncomfortable, and our natural tendency is to
reduce its intensity and duration.

Most of us react reflexively to physical pain. We want to
alleviate it as much as possible so that we can feel good again.
To do this we might seek any number of remedies or self-med-
ications. Whether we reach for a bandage, an ice pack, an
aspirin, or a glass of wine, our intention is to stop the pain.

Generally speaking, men are more likely than women to
place themselves in dangerous situations or participate in activities that could result in physical pain. Men are often encouraged to engage in risky behaviors to test their manhood, and
many actively seek danger as a way of proving themselves.
Years of socialization and conditioning mean that men are
tight-lipped when it comes to expressing their pain. It's a rare
man who will stay away from the office because of illness or
who will miss the Friday night softball game because of a
bruised shoulder.

Women tend to have fewer qualms about seeing a physician
or nurse when they need medical attention. They are not intol-

erant of pain; they are intolerant of unnecessary suffering. Many men, on the other hand, are reluctant to see a doctor or seek medical help. When injured or sick, men devise their own ways of treating their physical pain. Over-the-counter medications, long showers, an extra drink or two at lunch, or just "gutting it out" are ways that men work through their pain rather than confronting the source of it directly.

Many men handle emotional pain the same way they handle physical pain: feelings of sadness, disappointment, guilt, and fear are controlled and kept private. When the source of pain is not all that serious, these sorts of coping strategies can be effective. But when the source of pain is a major trauma like death or serious illness, such strategies may no longer work. The sense of destruction and disorientation men feel in the wake of tragedy may be too intense to cover up and control. While men may secretly wish they could look outside themselves for help or support, they may be so unwilling to admit defeat that they grit their teeth and vow to heal themselves on their own.

Men are problem solvers. To men, an illness, a death, or a major loss is just another problem to solve, and problems always have workable solutions. Very often, the solutions men fall back on are the ones they are most familiar with: repression, suppression, and denial.

Denial allows men to reduce their emotional pain, if not eliminate it all together. With the pressure turned down a notch or two, men may feel that things are under control again. The crisis, at least for the moment, is over, so why talk about it anymore? With their emotions in check, they go about the business of caring for their family or managing their daily affairs. But as pointed out in the earlier chapter on denial, feelings of grief are not so easily appeased.

Grief packs a punch. It doesn't just blow through like a sudden breeze that is here and then gone. It strikes like a tornado, destroying everything in sight. And the destruction is felt for months, even years. Any attempt at denying the intensity or duration of grief is unlikely to be successful over time.

Most of us become increasingly desperate when our usual repertoire of stress-reducing behaviors fails or when our emotional problems continue to escalate. To diminish the pain, some men, and women, turn to any number of addictive substances or addictive behaviors as a coping strategy. Some see alcohol as a way of anesthetizing their pain, while others escape by becoming occupied by an extramarital affair. The motivation is to find some outside diversion to occupy the mind and avoid the dismal work of grieving.

Today's society has often been labeled an addictive society because so many people rely on substances or activities to manage their stress and emotional pain. Alcohol, drugs, food, sex, gambling, work, and exercising can all potentially become components of addictive behavior. Indeed, any behavior that produces desirable results or gives relief from pain can become addictive. While it is possible to use addictive behaviors to relieve pain temporarily, engaging in compulsive acts or using addictive substances can force people into a downward spiral of addiction. Over time, addictions demand more and more attention while giving less and less relief. Although grief may be quieted for a while, the relief does not usually last long.

Addictive behaviors are substitutes for reality, for intimacy, for authenticity. The good feelings they mechanically invoke can lead to a false sense of security. Drinking beer always leaves us feeling mellow; eating an extra helping of dessert consistently brings us a sense of comfort and satiation; jogging through the park inevitably gives us a runner's high. These feelings differ significantly from the feelings we have when our friends stop asking how things are going, or our relatives criticize us for taking too long to get over our grief, or our boss suddenly expects us to be back to our old self on the job. Drugs, food, or money sometimes seem the only dependable means that we have for feeling better while we are grieving. This may be especially true for men, who are less likely than women to have multiple sources of emotional support. For men, another try at the roulette wheel, a few more hours at the office, or an extra pill now and then may be all they need to stop the pain. Addictive behaviors ease the longing and suffering men feel inside.

The basis of addictive behavior is the pursuit of pleasure. Not surprisingly, alcohol is the drug of choice for many men who want to numb their pain quickly and in a socially acceptable manner. A few drinks at night or a quick stop at the liquor store can round off the hard edge of reality. Some men say their drinking began or worsened because of a personal tragedy; others are merely continuing a long history of use—and abuse. Social drinking provides a good excuse to get out of the house and away from painful memories. A bar can provide anonymity or the company of friends who won't pry. Who can blame a man for stopping off for a drink or two after a trying day at the office? Alcohol replaces the pain and responsibilities of the home with a much more pleasant and peaceful atmosphere.

Like men, women use alcohol to relieve their emotional pain. Yet, women who use drugs or alcohol can pay a heftier price in depression, shame, and guilt. It's simply not as socially appropriate for a woman to drink heavily or frequently, so she may drink more in private to hide her addiction.

The vulnerable state that grief leaves us in almost always challenges our sexuality. Often, partners have very different sexual needs when they are grieving. Women, particularly, may feel so emotionally and physically fatigued that they are reluctant to be sexual with their partners, and they prefer to be comforted in less physical ways. Men may want sex, not to feel loved, but to contain or to escape their own vulnerable feelings and the pressures of intimacy. Sometimes these opposing needs are met by anonymous sex with multiple partners or an extramarital affair. For men, these sexual encounters may bring excitement, a sense of conquest, or a rush of power. They may feel free and temporarily immune to stress and anxiety. Women typically have affairs to feel wanted by someone unconnected to their grief. Sexual acting-out is not about caring and love, it is about finding an instant fix to one's fears, tensions, and emptiness.

Couples who are experiencing infertility or who have suffered a miscarriage, stillbirth, or infant death are almost certain to have conflicts over sex. The passion to have a baby or to replace a child who has died can easily turn to desperation when months or even years of trying are met with repeated failures. Genuine intimacy can get blurred, and lovemaking is reduced to a singular, obsessive goal. As the biological clock keeps ticking, women, especially, become more frantic and demanding in their desire for sexual relations. Compulsive sex depersonalizes partners, leaving them feeling empty and alone. Difficult, too, for some men and women is the incompatibility of physical pleasure and grieving—of life versus death.

Work is the ultimate escape for many men. The duties and responsibilities of a career take time and concentration, and many men let their work preoccupy and consume them. The job leaves little time to think about a father's death, a horrifying car accident, or a child's illness. Working harder and longer means men can absent themselves physically and mentally from their family. There is a legitimate reason not to be home, not to have time to talk about the tragedy, not to deal with the family's needs. The job becomes a place to lose oneself and escape one's pain.

In their desperation to escape their pain, many grieving men do more than just become absorbed in their work—they make their career their life. Work defines them. It becomes the sole measure of their worth and the sole supplier of their needs. It takes precedence over everyone and everything, from family, friends, and relatives to eating, sleeping, and relaxing. These men believe that success on the job proves they are still capable, while absolving them of responsibility for the death, loss, or personal tragedy they and their family have had to endure. Richard Friberg's workaholic behaviors were his solution to being fired. Unwilling to allow another job to control him, he let work become his life.

Some workaholic men try to mold themselves into indispensable employees. They strive to be their company's all-time top sales associate or their school's Teacher of the Year. They want to be more than just another valued employee; they want to be the very best, most esteemed employee in the company. To accomplish this, they set unrealistic goals, control decision-making dictatorially, and refuse to delegate responsibilities. Their real goal is not to do something valuable and meaningful, but to ensure that they will never be abandoned by their employer.

Addictive behaviors have a way of flourishing when we grieve. Our abilities to view our actions with insight and to practice self-restraint are weakened by grief. Our beliefs and values may feel a little shaky, too. The momentary high we gain from winning a bet at the racetrack or working out at the gym can take on disproportionate significance when contrasted with the drudgery of grieving. The diversion is exciting, and the relief feels good. Forgotten are the memories, the people, and the places that have caused us so much pain. Once ignited, the spark of euphoria can flame into an unquenchable fire of desire.

Addictions and addictive behaviors are empty sources of pleasure. Alcohol, drugs, sex, money, or gambling are incapable of sustaining us physically, emotionally, intellectually, or spiritually over any length of time. Addictions eventually enslave us, demanding more and more of our time, money, sanity, and health while offering less and less fulfillment and pleasure. Men who attempt to manage their grief by engaging in addictive behaviors run the risk of becoming ensnared in the vicious cycle of addiction, a far greater problem than the one they are trying to solve.

Fortify your heart

Addictive behaviors are deceitful. The pleasures they bring can fool men into believing that they are not as needy and vulnerable as they really are. Lost in the addictive behavior is the truth of the emotional pain the man feels, and his need for others. Many men rely on alcohol, work, drugs, sex, gambling, or other addictive substances and activities to escape and forget their pain. Any challenge or threat women make to such behavior is met with resistance, justifications, or blame. Women must see the truth of addiction—the craziness and irrationality it creates. They must protect themselves from its deceptions by fortifying their heart. A strong heart resists falsehoods.

Women tend to focus on emotions when they are grieving. Their first inclination is to look at life through the prism of the heart. Men tend to look on grieving from a very different perspective. Life, for many men, is about solving problems and strategizing for success. Addictive substances and behaviors give men the illusion of power and control. The seductive power of addiction is slow, but deliberate.

Addictive behaviors can be highly destructive, especially when they become patterned and well-entrenched. For many women, their partner's addiction is a second loss. Fearful and insecure, these women may feel threatened emotionally and even physically. Their natural tendency is to try to control their partner. Failing that, they may begin to question their own reality. That is what co-dependency is all about: one dysfunctional behavior reinforcing another. What women in this situation need more than anything is truth and inner strength.

A woman can find inner strength in the depths of her own soul. She can fortify her heart by discovering her own emotional reality—a reality that honestly claims her fears, doubts, and desires rather than denying or distorting them. When a woman stands tall in her own truth, she is better prepared to handle the deceptions of her partner's addiction.

9

Despair

Each day ends at its beginning,
Crouched over a newspaper and sour coffee,
A robe for a suit. My thumbs blackened
On pages of tiny script, hope smattered
Across recycled pulp. It all turns to
Garbage, mixed with rotting aspirations.
I've collected too many wrinkles to fit,
But I'm too restless to sleep.

—Louis Cerulli

Caught in a Golden Parachute

It felt like everything was falling apart. The man I had counted as my best friend in life had fired me. Sure, it was at the direction of the new owners, but that didn't alleviate the pain. My friends and I had started the company, and now I was being shuffled out of the way because my position was expendable. My buddies made absolutely great software products, and the new management could still use their creative talents. I was the company president, and with new management came new leaders. No one cared that I had helped make the company a success, they just tossed me aside and continued on without me.

The parachute they gave me before letting me go was definitely golden. I had been fired without cause, and so, by contract, I had to be paid for the next two years. I would get a low six-figure income that would allow me to sleep late and watch the afternoon soaps. I suppose I should have been cheering and getting out the brochures for Hawaii. Instead, I felt as if I were in a nightmare from which I could not wake up.

Not working was incredibly hard on me, but I tried not to let my feelings show. I kept all of my emotions locked in a mental box, with the debris of my botched job, a divorce, Vietnam, and every other difficult time in my life piled up inside. I was no psychologist, but I'd had enough practical explosives training to know that opening up all of this emotional "stuff" required the know-how of experienced folks, or parts of me might start flying in every direction. Unwilling to risk an emotional explosion, I was stuck with no job and a feeling of failure.

Having a job seemed to be my birthright. I had grown up in a rural Kansas town where hard work was looked upon as a manly virtue and sloth was not to be tolerated. I'd had my first paper route at the age of eight and had always held at least one job since 1948. Growing up in a small town, where the serious country could be found five minutes in any direction, meant that bragging rights were won by how much hay had been hauled or how many acres had been plowed. Now, jobless, I was struggling to regain my identity. Still, my ideas of a man, based on role models from my youth, taught me to be stoic and to endure.

It didn't take long for depression to set in. I had no idea that so much of my self-image was dependent on what I did to bring home a paycheck. Finding out was shocking, and damn scary. My gut twisted into a knot. I cried for the first time since I was eleven, but I was careful not to let anyone see my tears. I cried only when I was alone, usually at daybreak after a sleepless night. In the early morning, it seemed that I was the only living thing awake in the universe. At these hours, any noise from the street was a welcome sound.

Turning all my sadness, anger, and confusion inward left me with an incredible feeling of despair. As they say in the Navy, I was at the "Atlantic trough, white whaleshit level."

Despite everything, I decided to try to find another job. I sent copies of my résumé to business contacts whose names I had obtained from friends and the business press, but I got little response. Those few businesses that did contact me made up excuses for not hiring me. I was "out of the loop," they claimed. I had been away from their market for too long, building my software firm, to be successful in their business.

I began to lose steam as rejection after rejection piled up in front of me. In desperation, I tried calling some of my former business associates who had, in the past, guaranteed that I would always be welcome in their companies. When they didn't return my calls either, I felt total despair.

My failure to locate work took its toll on me. I was officially diagnosed with depression. All the emotional stuff I had kept locked inside me caused my stomach to fill with acid. I began using prescription drugs to enhance my moods and wearing a TMJ splint to stop the annoying pain in my jaws. I was convinced that I had somehow miffed some ancient divinity, and in retaliation had had a curse put on my head.

Over the last nine years, I have continued to suffer from the pain of being fired from my job. My wife has been supportive, but I don't often discuss my feelings with her. I just can't open that box full of emotions that holds all of the residue of my past failures. I don't know any other way to deal with this kind of grief. I follow the example of my childhood role models back in Kansas: I "shut up and go on."

—Jim Murrow

All of us want to know that our life counts for something. We need some validation that we contribute to the world in a significant way. Having meaning in life helps us feel satisfied and secure with ourselves and with others.

The meaning of life is not something we can order from a home-shopping network or find indexed in the yellow pages. It is something we must create out of our own life experience. It is what we labor for at home and work. It is what we seek in our relationships with others. Meaning comes from a personal appraisal of all the accumulated moments of one's life—the joyful and fulfilling moments as well as the painful and disheartening moments.

So much of how we construct meaning is shaped by our interactions with others. We want friendships, love, connectedness. Most of us actively seek out the companionship of others. Our desire, typically, is to interact with another person in such a way as to bring pleasure and meaning to both of our lives. This is why we get impatient and annoyed by superficial, pointless, or hurtful encounters. And this is why we feel secure and happy when we do make a meaningful connection with another person.

Feeling secure in the world gives us a place of belonging. That place of belonging exists inside us as much as outside us. When we find a place of belonging, our level of energy and vitality for life can soar. There is a grounding and connectedness that comes from knowing that we have attachments to people, things, and activities in the world. The security we feel encourages us to be flexible in mind and spirit, open to life.

From a sense of security flows goodwill—a concept that most of us would define in terms of the golden rule: "Do unto others as you would have others do unto you." We see respect, kindness, and charity as values of the heart and believe that these values are integral to our identity and integrity. These values guide our behaviors, attitudes, and actions. They give us a sense of purpose and kindle a warmth in our spirit. Most of us expect our goodwill to strengthen relationships, and we trust that the process of knowing, loving, and relating to others will change us for the better. We find comfort in knowing and being known.

Knowing and being known by others gives us an understanding of intimacy and the power to influence our surroundings. It also helps us learn the importance of values and how they govern our life. Values shape who we are and how we act. They define what it means to love and be loved, and, like moral traffic cops, they direct us as we move from moment to moment, place to place, in our everyday lives.

Values enhance our clarity and sense of purpose. Most of us want to know where we stand ethically in the world, and we derive great assurance in knowing that we are doing the right thing. We want to know what is expected of us so that we can take appropriate actions, make reasonable decisions, or choose wisely between options.

Personal tragedy feels like a sudden and incomprehensible violation of our value system. As was the case with Jim Murrow's abrupt departure from his company, an unexpected loss can render our life's compass useless and leave us wandering hopelessly in search of meaning and clarity.

There is no simple explanation for why tragedies occur. Neither can we know in advance how we will react to a tragedy if and when one occurs. We depend on our values to make sense of the world, but, when tragedy strikes, even our most basic values may seem pointless and ineffective. What once made sense no longer does, and we can be thrown into a crisis of despair.

Many men describe despair as a pervasive sense of darkness, an almost hellish pit of discouragement, despondency, and hopelessness. As hellish as this pit is, some men find they cannot avoid it. Once grief has destroyed their purpose in life, they haven't the strength to keep from falling into despair.

Like bitterness, despair is marked by a slow descent into an emotional prison. The descent begins as men sense that their efforts to stave off grief are feeble and useless. Attempts to rationalize the situation fail, and life slips increasingly out of control.

As the grieving man descends into despair, he is overcome by a tiredness of spirit, and even speech becomes difficult. To feel despair is to be apathetic, listless, and inert. Under the weight of his grief, the man's very identity crumbles; he begins to loathe himself and doubt his own ability to survive. Hope becomes an illusion; life seems mean and worthless.

Men, as a rule, want—and expect—life to be coherent and logical. But grief brings with it only incoherency and illogic. Suddenly, there is no job to drive to every morning, no father to visit at Christmastime, no cherished child to comfort after a bad day. Instead, there is only an aching heart and a mind oversaturated with conflicting thoughts. In the chaos of grief, there are few standards that men can use to measure and demonstrate their worth. Inevitably, they begin to wonder if they have any worth at all.

Most men want to leave a mark on the world, to produce something of value that will outlive them. When grief robs a man of his self-worth, however, it robs him of his legacy as well, for how can a man who is worthless produce anything of lasting value? For the grieving man, life suddenly changes from a place of challenge and opportunity to one of peril and fear. He can no longer trust his world or anything in it.

When trust erodes, many men retreat into a state of intense inwardness. They reject the outside world and its agendas and demands. The discomfort they feel depletes them of desire, and their life energy slowly dissipates. In the struggle to understand what has happened to them, men isolate themselves emotionally. Believing that things are never going to improve, they may project a strange sense of calmness and resignation.

Women are not exempt from despair. Because they place so much importance on intimacy and connectedness, any significant loss of affection can become a prescription for despair. This is especially true when a child dies or when there is a crisis involving childbearing. In such cases, women can come to feel enveloped in alienation and depression. They are unsure of how to continue on with their lives now that roles they had anticipated for themselves seem illusory or threatened. In waking hours and nighttime dreams, they wonder if they are still a mother, a best friend, or a lovable person.

As with other emotional issues, men and women do not always express their depression similarly. While both men and women may exhibit such obvious symptoms as extreme changes in daily habits and routines, loss of pleasure, apathy, fatigue, disorganization, and a lack of concentration, some men may conceal their depression behind a wall of quiet desperation. While they may insist that nothing is wrong, inside these men are seething, ready to explode at the slightest provocation. Behind the facade of competence and normalcy, these men hide a secret depression.

For some men, depression comes like a magician with a bag of tricks: its symptoms are apparent one day only to disappear the next. Men wonder if they have just had a bad day or perhaps are catching a bug. Because they are uncertain what's happening to them, they try to keep going and pretend that nothing is wrong. To admit that they are depressed would mean embracing the reality of their pain and the humiliation of not being man enough to handle their problems.

Depression is very common in grieving, with both genders reporting some lowering of mood. Men, more than women, however, feel that they must overcome the stigma of weakness associated with being depressed. Men are supposed to be invulnerable. Rather than admit their weakness and vulnerability, many men, out of shame, avoid seeking help. Consequently, their depression deepens, becoming more intractable. Shame only makes men feel defective and offers no relief from self-loathing.

The stigma of depression also affects women. Their partner's depressed mood is worrisome to them. Some women want to protect their partner by colluding to keep his depression a secret. They minimize his low mood and provide ready excuses to family and friends about his declining ability to function normally. Other women fear what their partner's depression means for the survival of their relationship. Afraid that confronting their partner will only make things worse, they help conceal the depression by saying nothing about it.

When depressed, both men and women tend to obsess on the negatives and lose sight of life's positives. They may complain, for example, that they have lost their sense of taste or smell, or that life is drab and colorless. Optimism is replaced by feelings of helplessness. When a man, in particular, begins to question his ability to shape the future, he may also begin to question whether his life is still worth living. Exhausted by his suffering, he may entertain thoughts of suicide as a way to escape his pain and minimize the burden on his family.

Despair directs men away from hope and toward self-destruction. It convinces them that the world is hostile and holds no satisfying meaning. Until men can find new meaning—and rediscover hope—their life will seem purposeless and empty.

Foster hope

Men and women both understand that it is natural to feel angry, disoriented, or fearful while grieving, although women tend to be less hesitant about talking and working through their grief with others. Neither men nor women want their grief to become chronic or debilitating, to drag them down into despair. Despair is an ugly, dark place that saps people of their life energy and causes them to reject love, comfort, and goodness. To counteract this rejection, women must foster hope in their own ability to adapt to life and create new meaning and purpose for themselves. They can then encourage their partner to do the same.

Despair threatens the intimate bond between a woman and her partner. Rather than feeling hopeless about this threat, the woman needs to work hard to nurture new opportunities and dreams. She needs to locate those sources of satisfaction, pleasure, and beauty that still exist in her relationship. We can all feel good about something, and we will need to look inward to those strengths we do possess, that support we can muster, that faith we still hold on to.

Hope sustains us. It motivates us to act when we might otherwise remain immobile. It is hope that finally pushes us out of the house after weeks of self-imposed exile or gives us the strength to be intimate with our partner after grief has left us disinterested in sex. Hope is an integral part of any relationship. It illuminates the possibilities in life and encourages us to expand our understanding of who we are, individually and as partners. It is not easy to find hope after a significant loss. Yet hope is an essential part of healing.

PART THREE

PROSPECTS FOR RENEWAL

10

A Time of Change
and Healing

Awake in mourning's garden, I sow
Pain in uneven rows, pulling weeds from
Between my feet. I bury hardship under
Hibiscus, it steeps the soil in sweat,
Roots itself under my soles
Until I kneel under a corpulent moon.
I steal its borrowed light, pull it through my
Pores and madness becomes lucidity.

—Louis Cerulli

Choosing Happiness over Sorrow

Several years ago, as I was driving on a two-lane road, a school bus approached me from another direction. The bus moved into a turn lane, did not stop at the intersection, and hit me. My pickup truck was damaged, and my lower back was badly injured.

I was left in great physical pain—unable ever to go horseback riding, skiing, or white-water rafting again, or to play football or baseball with friends. I had to go to the doctor for frequent medical tests, and I endured physical therapy that brought tears of pain to my eyes.

Questions plagued me. Would I ever be able to work again? If I returned to work, would my job still be there? Would I be able to perform my work at the same level as before my injury? How would my fellow employees react to me? (I could no longer walk normally.) How would I react to my fellow employees? (My chronic pain made me irritable.)

After many months, I was able to return to work, but only part-time.

Because of the heavy medication I took for pain during my rehabilitation, I could not drive a car. One morning a coworker, Gail, picked me up and drove me to work. Getting out of the car was physically difficult. As I walked down the long corridor to my office, I took baby steps. That was all I could take. As Gail was holding my upper arm to support me, I began sobbing. Gail thought the physical pain was making me cry, but I was crying because I thought that I would be this way for the rest of my life. I was afraid. Gail took me to her office, where I calmed down. After regaining my composure, I began my day at work.

In my experience, pain amplifies stress. There were times at work when I just closed my office door and cried. Then I could go on with what I needed to do. Even though this was not the sort of behavior that society promotes for men, crying made me feel better. I needed to grieve for all those things I was losing.

My friends helped me survive. They would send cookies or call to see how I was doing. They would bring me chocolate milkshakes when the pain was especially bad. I appreciated their honest responses to my terrible situation—for example, when they would admit, "I don't even know what to say." Even so, at times I wanted to isolate myself because I felt ashamed of the condition I was in. I did not feel like a complete person. I felt unworthy of their friendship and love. My friends, though, stayed with me.

My physical pain eventually became easier to bear. Through physical therapy, I became more mobile and could focus my mind on aspects of my life other than pain. I believed that my body would return to the way it was before the accident, but every doctor I went to told me something along the lines of "You'll have to live with it." No physician could fix my back.

I realized I had to change my focus from "getting well" to adapting to my new reality. Instead of daydreaming about what I could not do, I had to start focusing on what I could do. I decided to get on with my life. My hope had to come from within me.

As a way to cope and grieve, I kept a journal in the months after my accident. I had not done much writing previously. In my journal, I wrote about how each day went and how I felt. I wrote about my despair, my thoughts about spirituality, and my thoughts about people. I wrote down my prayers. Once I decided to change my outlook from despair to hope, I reread what I'd written. Through my own words, I saw that I had improved a lot. I had survived the worst, and I was recovering. Though my memory of the accident was still strong, my memories of the pain had diminished with time.

I do not believe in the common notion that "good things come out of bad things." I do believe, though, that I had choices to make because of my injury. I could have committed suicide, but I didn't. Suicide only widens the circle of pain. I know because my oldest brother committed suicide.

I chose hope and faith in God. Though it was not always clear to me when I was suffering the most, I did really want to live my life in happiness rather than in sorrow. Though most of the sports I had enjoyed were not mine to do anymore, I could go fly-fishing. I could catch fish again. That, in itself, gave me happiness. I started doing volunteer work, helping others through their difficult times. That also gave me happiness, as well as more patience and a deeper understanding of what faith and love had in common.

Before the accident, I had felt that my life had a purpose. I decided I wanted my life after the accident—my new life—to have a purpose, too.

—Thomas Chalfant

Life is a continuous series of beginnings and endings. Whether it is the sun rising and setting, a school year beginning and ending, or a house being sold and a new one purchased, life is punctuated by starts and stops. Some of these beginnings and endings—birth and death, for example—are more significant than others, but all are woven tightly into the very essence of our being. The changes heralded by beginnings and endings fill our days, weeks, months, and years. Sometimes change is exciting and challenging; other times, it invites dread or misery. Little in life stays the same, and there is a beginning and ending to almost everything.

Many beginnings and endings are marked by tradition or celebration. These traditions establish a context for honoring and acknowledging change. New Year's Day, May Day, and Thanksgiving inform us of the passage of time and the movement from one season to another. The many religious holidays, like Christmas, Hanukkah, Passover, Good Friday, and Easter also designate important beginnings and endings for those of faith. Ceremonies like weddings, graduations, the christening of a baby, wakes, and funerals all lend formal significance, and a sense of reverence, to important transitions in our life.

Some of the starts and stops we encounter in life take place without major fanfare and occur quite naturally. Many of these are internal changes that test our ability to adapt and grow. Moving from childhood to adolescence to adulthood, and throughout our adult years, we change priorities, purpose, values, and beliefs. So, too, wisdom replaces our youthful exuberance as we see our dreams and hopes tested by reality.

As our roles and life patterns vary, our connections to people, places, events, activities also vary. Friends come and go; relationships once intimate and vital wither away and are replaced with others that hold a new, albeit different, significance. The birth of a child, our first home, a new job, relocation to a new city—any of these might call for a reordering of life and a reinventing of our selves. Though initially we may protest loudly, most of us see these stops and starts as a necessary evolution in defining and creating who we are.

Life isn't always about such essential transitions and changes. Sometimes it's the little comings and goings in our life that encourage us and nurture our capacity to grow. Perhaps it's feeling the freedom that comes with being barefoot and barelegged on the first truly hot day of summer, or finally feeling brave enough to venture onto the Internet without help. It may be the willingness to volunteer for an important project at the office, or allowing ourselves the luxury of taking a trip alone for the first time. These beginnings may seem small and almost inconsequential, but they are a start toward something new and a helpful reminder that we have cause to feel hopeful about life.

Though beginnings and endings often signify hope and promise, many of us approach them with trepidation. Change can be difficult. Transitions induce periods of discomfort as we try to reestablish balance and harmony. Nowhere is the proposition of change more daunting than when we are grieving the death of someone we love or the loss of something important in our life. At these times, change feels like a monumental task.

There is no doubt that grieving takes enormous energy. The realization that every aspect of our life has changed profoundly is difficult to comprehend. Not only must we cope with our emotional suffering, but, like Thomas Chalfant, we must work to restructure our life patterns. Day-to-day routines must be reestablished. So much of what characterized our life may have ended or may no longer feel comfortable or appropriate.

It is painful to think about how our connections to the people, places, activities, and things that were once so familiar—the nurse who always seemed to know what to say, the friendly coffee shop we frequented on our route to work, or our child's school and classmates—have been irrevocably altered.

One dilemma in grieving is knowing what parts of our life we can salvage and what parts we need to discard. We are plagued with worry about our ability to get behind the wheel of a car again. We wonder if we will ever be able to thumb through our family album without sobbing. Then, too, we are confused about the plans we had for the future. What do we do about our dreams to travel, to work abroad for a year, to learn to play the flute, to land that one big sales account, to volunteer more at church? Sorting out our roles, expectations, motivations, and desires can feel quite discouraging. The death of our dreams and hopes is anguishing.

In most cases, the endings and beginnings that cause us to grieve are thrust upon us without any choice. We don't expect our life to be shattered, and we naturally feel helpless and unprepared when tragedy strikes. Trying to heal ourselves and go on with our lives is a tortuous battle.

To heal from a significant loss requires will power, intentionality, a conscious decision to work at getting better. It is not something that can be left to chance. It certainly won't happen overnight, and it will never happen without real effort, as Thomas Chalfant eventually learned. If we throw seeds carelessly about a garden plot, we probably won't have much to harvest in the fall. But if we plan out our garden, carefully tilling, preparing, and seeding the soil, there is a much better chance that our harvest will be abundant. Time can heal some wounds, but finding true peace means facing uncertainty and taking risks.

Sometimes, in women's eyes, the ways in which men grieve seem to be less about healing grief than avoiding it. Certainly, behaviors such as anger, control, addiction, denial, and bitterness are more suggestive of efforts to ignore or contain grief than to address it directly. Yet the process of grieving isn't all that clear-cut, and what may appear dysfunctional or maladaptive to one person may be, to some degree, beneficial for another. As previous chapters have shown, men work very hard at coping with grief, though often in very different ways than women. Healing doesn't always come in large, grand leaps for men, but often in short, incremental steps.

Men, like women, know that they need to reestablish their life patterns after a loss. They realize that they have to find a way to function in the present, reinventing a self that is different from both the self they were in the past and the self they thought they would be in the future. They also know that there are choices to make about how to deal with grief. Many men can accept what has happened to them. Their challenge, however, is to go beyond merely accepting a loss to embracing the opportunities it offers for change and growth.

Because men often think of themselves as builders and fixers, they tend to be very sensitive to the destruction that grief causes—the stresses on the family, friendships, finances, career. These are things men want to repair and get in order, and their controlling, angry, denying, bitter, or addictive behaviors can be seen as attempts to reconstruct the world in order to restore some sense of security and predictability to life. By attempting to repair these problems, men feel they are living up to their responsibilities and duties.

Even though they may tackle their problems immediately, many men are slow to accept the full reality of a personal tragedy. Some try to minimize the importance of a loss by letting denial numb out the truth. Others anesthetize themselves with addictive behaviors or succumb to depression or despair. For some, attempts to hide from the truth may last until the initial crisis is under control; others stay in denial for years. In these latter cases especially, men may find that delaying their grieving has badly disrupted their relationships with other people. Healing starts when men begin to restore their relationships and work to establish a more functional identity, one that integrates their old self with their new self.

Even when it becomes clear that they need to redefine themselves, men may face the task with great reluctance. Anger hasn't stopped their pain, denial isn't working anymore, despair and depression have only complicated matters. Admitting that they can't defeat this thing is humbling. Surrender is never easy for men.

Surrendering to grief may be less difficult for women, who tend to see it as less an issue of ego and power than a matter of necessity. Grief disintegrates the self. Therefore, healing requires finding concrete ways to incorporate past roles and responsibilities into a new identity. Wholeness comes by combining what was and what can be in a way that creates a self that still honors the past. In this way, the past is not abandoned or destroyed but, like a house that still has value, reconstructed, refurbished, renovated. Women continue to fill the roles of mother, worker, and caretaker despite the loss of a child, career, or parent.

Men know that they can no longer trust their assumptions about how the world ought to be and they desperately want life to make sense again. To find new meaning, they are forced to reexamine their core beliefs about fairness, justice, truth, and respect. Such intense self-examination can lead men to reframe their thoughts and emotions about their loss and eventually to formulate new assumptions about the world. These new assumptions can take many forms—that the world is an untrustworthy place, that life is fleeting and every moment counts, that men can depend on others to help them. Whatever conclusions they reach, men are attempting to heal by putting their tragedy into a meaningful perspective.

As men try to redefine their world and their self, they may also think through issues of faith and spirituality. Many may wrestle with their anger and wonder why they weren't spared from suffering. Measuring their life against the lives of others, they may blame God for their tragedy and even call into question their most fundamental religious beliefs. They may question the use of being faithful when God doesn't seem to care about them. For some, the incessant thoughts of "Why me, why now, why not someone else?" finally yield answers. These men choose to build a new relationship with their God or discover other ways to develop a spiritual life.

The emotional upheaval men experience after the death of a loved one or other significant loss is considerable, no matter how much they may try to disguise it. Men often hide behind anger, denial, and controlling behaviors, and in the shadows of despair and depression. Many reserve their grieving for private times and private places. Fearful of how others will react, many men prefer to grieve alone, to weep and mourn in the privacy of their own soul.

Society has made grieving doubly hard on men. For one thing, it has given men few, if any, words to express their feelings, even though their emotions are as intense as those of their partner. Second, even if they were able to articulate their pain, most men lack a safe environment in which to share their feelings. Rather, they feel pressured to keep everything buttoned up inside or to search out opportunities to grieve in solitude. Many men would be more expressive if they did not feel that they would be violating their masculinity in the process. Like women, men want to be understood in their grief and want the freedom to grieve in their own way.

The lack of safety men feel is sometimes difficult for women to understand. Women see safety as a natural extension of intimacy—a right or entitlement of a committed partnership. To think that their partner does not feel safe enough to share feelings is shocking and disconcerting. Yet many men do not feel they have their partner's permission to be vulnerable. Rather than feeling that intimacy is a two-way street, men often experience it as a setting where their deepest needs may be ridiculed and ignored. Without a genuine sense that they are safe, men will have trouble summoning the courage to heal or making real advances in transforming their lives and relationships.

As healing drives men to reexperience and realize the truth of their connectedness to others, they learn what many women have known all along about intimacy. They begin to understand that they, too, depend on intimacy, that they, too, have a hunger to feel wanted, loved, and cared about. Such insights help both genders recognize that, though their actions may be very different, their felt experiences are very similar.

Hidden in their pain and misery, many men find opportunities to redefine themselves, to reprioritize and enrich their life. Finding a new purpose in life is an enormous undertaking, but with time many men are able to pursue what matters most in their hearts.

Search out new truths

Life is filled with uncertainty after the death of a loved one or other catastrophic loss. Knowing how to go on is difficult, particularly when so much of what was familiar has now been wiped away. The choice to heal is not any easier for women than it is for men. Each must dig deep in their souls for the resolve to forge ahead. Loss calls into question one's existence, purpose in life, goals—one's truths. To heal, women must search out new truths about their partner's grief and about their own struggles. In so doing, they will find reasons to survive.

This search for new truths brings women face to face with all the realities of tragedy—emptiness, loneliness, despair, and the uncertainty of whether happiness will ever be possible again. Ultimately, this search requires women to address deep-seated fears about their partner's love and their chances for renewing their intimate partnership.

The work of grieving sometimes appears to be endless. Yet, though there may be times when women feel emotionally exhausted, they must continue to make room in their heart for their partner, accepting him for where he is, not where he should be. As women learn more about how their partner grieves, they can begin to recognize what they should and should not expect from him. Any perceptions that the man is uncaring diminish when women empathize rather than criticize. Taking the risk to expose the hurts in their own heart allows women to appreciate those things that make their intimate partnership so important. Women want the best for their partners and themselves. With compassion and persistence, they can learn invaluable lessons about love.

11

Transformations

Raw on a cliff, a rock
Sits ragged under the sky. Years
Wash its shell with torrents and
Winds that massage its hide until
Shadows melt from its emerging curves,
Warmed in beams from an unknown
Dawn, the impenetrable releases its sculpture,
Ever-changing, always becoming itself.

—Louis Cerulli

The Circle of Grief

It has been more than eight years since the accident. Once or twice a year I drive over the bridge and up the winding road to look at the ditch where Jason died. I drive to the television station where he worked, so I can turn around and drive back that last stretch of road he ever saw. I come up on the turn, and I still cannot understand how he got off the road and onto the shoulder, but the logic of what happened next is tragically transparent. The first few times I returned, I could see the gouged earth, the glass, and other debris. Nature has since smoothed the gouges, and tall grass hides the debris. Nature does not work so quickly on the human heart.

In a few weeks, I will be fifty years old. Had he lived, my son Jason would be twenty-seven.

I am better now than I was. I have had help from family and friends, from dreams, and from the drama and drudgery of everyday life. It is easy to become preoccupied with the tasks of living. I have tried to help myself. At first I did this by writing. I kept a personal journal; I wrote about my experiences, thoughts, and feelings. I wrote of pain, death, and life. It was therapeutic, and, eventually, I revised my journal into a book, The Fall of a Sparrow: Of Death and Dreams and Healing.

I have also created rituals to commemorate Jason's life, to remind me of his presence and to symbolize my love for him. If I see a coin on the ground, I pick it up, and I save it until the next time I visit the cemetery. I put the coins I have found on the monument, next to Jason's name. Jason was careless with money; he was always losing change. I often saw coins on the floor of his car or his room. If I find coins now, it's as if Jason is still alive, losing money, and it is my job as a father to return his money to him.

My wife, too, has rituals. Each time she visits the cemetery, she kisses her fingers and brushes them against the picture of Jason on his stone, and says out loud, "I love you, Jason. I miss you." She keeps some of Jason's sweaters in a drawer, and wears one when she is missing him the most. Every Christmas she decorates a small tree, and together we put it by his grave.

During the first Christmas season after Jason's death, I went to the cemetery almost every day. On one visit I noticed ticket stubs from a local movie theater stuck onto some of the tree's branches. Jason and his friends loved films, so I was certain that some of his friends had stopped at the cemetery on their way back from a movie. I liked the idea. I began bringing my ticket stubs and attaching them to the tree. After we took the Christmas tree down, I stuck stubs inside a small ceramic dog that stands by his grave.

On the night Jason died, someone at the hospital gave me the backpack that Jason used for carrying his school books. Whenever my wife and I go for a long trip, we take that backpack with us. It is a way to pretend that Jason is with us.

These rituals—those that are public and those that are private—are satisfying. They have helped me heal. I am better now than I was.

Immediately after Jason's death, I had a period of numbness. When the numbness receded and the pain increased, I sometimes used alcohol to bring the numbness back. After each day at work, I would come home and write in my journal, desperately trying to capture my pain in words. After writing, I would watch television or read, but too many times I would open a bottle of wine and drink until the numbness returned. It was a bad idea, but it took a long time for me to be convinced that it was harming me more than it was helping me. Sometimes even the alcohol did not help, and then I would listen to songs that I knew would make me weep. The tears worked like a safety valve, releasing the pressure of the pain welling up in my heart.

I am better now than I was. For a long time after Jason's death, it still felt like the accident had happened "yesterday." Many months passed before it began to seem like the accident had happened "last week." Years passed before it began to feel like the accident had happened "last month." Now, eight years after Jason's death, it seems like the accident happened "a few months ago." This slow passage of my internal clock suggests how raw my wound is and how much it still hurts. It is also a measure, though, of my healing.

My healing has come from the rituals my wife and I have created: the coins, the sweaters, the Christmas trees, the ticket stubs, the backpack. My healing has come from the writing I have done—informally and formally—and from the stories about Jason I share orally with others. My healing has come from the openness with which my wife and I talk about Jason, including those times when grief washes over me in a rush of memory, regret, and tears.

My healing goes on, and so must my rituals. I am better now than I was.

Often, though, my mind races in circles, thinking about Jason. I wonder where he would be living and what he would be doing if he had not died when he was nineteen years old. When I see a movie, I wonder what Jason would have thought about it. I wonder if Jason would have fulfilled his dream of being able to make movies. My thoughts race around and around in this empty space in ever-widening circles.

I am better now than I was, but there is no antidote for grief. The son I loved is dead. That fact is as cold, hard, and permanent as the granite marking his grave. My grief is as permanent as that *stone on which my name is carved next to the names of my wife and my son. I grieve because I loved him. I will miss him until I am lying next to him.*

Jason loved life, and he would not want me to waste what is left of my life. He would want me to enjoy and appreciate what life offers. So I go on, grateful for the presence of my wife and daughter, saddened by the absence of my son, and embracing Jason's memory.

I know that my love for Jason is both cause and cure for my suffering if I use that love in the right way. Because I know that, I am better than I was.

—Kent L. Koppelman

All of us want to survive our loss and get better. We want more good days than bad, more things to look forward to than things to dread. After a loss, we yearn to feel again the energy and emotion of being fully alive. We have not forgotten the past. We never will. The past is the stuff the present is made of.

Coping with grief and surviving tragedy takes endurance. There is so much to learn and to relearn as we try to make sense of what has happened. Searching for all the pieces that will put our life back together takes time. Sadly, there are no guarantees that our partner will grieve and heal as we do. No two people grieve the same. No two people heal the same.

When we choose to do what it takes to heal ourselves, we open ourselves to possibilities and hope. It is as if doors long closed have suddenly opened wide, and we can now see the possibility of living a fuller, more authentic life and forging a stronger relationship with our partner. As we move forward, hope encourages us to take risks and to make more of our lives than we ever imagined.

So much of grieving and healing is about courage. It takes courage to find strength in the midst of helplessness and hopelessness. It takes courage to triumph over our fears and embrace living. It takes courage to integrate loss into our personal history and pursue new meaning in life.

Being courageous about grieving isn't the same as being heroic. Heroes inhabit the fantasy worlds of comic books, action movies, and romance novels—worlds in which the hero always wins. Heroes transform their world, their world doesn't transform them.

In the real world, grief transforms us all. The nature of this transformation is part of the challenge of grieving, of being courageous. If we are unwilling to face all that grieving throws at us, we may change only minimally, limping along in life, not really happy, but no longer sad. Those who make this choice rely on time to soothe over the raw spots and, they gradually accept that their life will never be the same. Life loses its meaning, but at least the grief lessens. They survive, but they don't thrive.

With courage, however, grief can radically transform life perspectives, and new growth can take root in the barren desert of mind and spirit. Courageous grievers face fears and the uncertainty of the future. They let go of the old for the promise of something new. They awaken to life rather than remaining paralyzed. Courageous grievers believe that life is worth living, even though they may have occasional doubts. They have stopped looking for the answer to why something bad happened to them. Instead, they accept that living is an imperfect process and that active grieving can eventually restore them to wholeness.

The transformations that men experience tend to take the form of subtle shifts in thinking, feeling, and acting. Initially, the shift may seem slight: a desire to spend less time at the office, a willingness to join in more family activities, a concern about one's spiritual life, an interest in joining a support group. Over time, however, the impact of this shift can grow, causing profound changes.

Transformations are more likely to come from quiet reflection than hasty judgments. Men who change out of knee-jerk reactions never quite succeed in finding inner peace. Their reactionary changes have little to do with conscious effort and more to do with crisis management and quick fixes.

True transformations are intentional actions. They are purposeful attempts to deal with the painful reality of a loss.

They are a desire for emotional, spiritual, cognitive, physical, and behavioral wholeness. Transformations are born of determination and a letting go of our old perspectives, expectations, and priorities.

The contemplative nature of transformation slowly warms men to new awarenesses about the people in their lives, their own behaviors and attitudes, and their world view. As they make the passage from the old to the new, many men begin to identify parts of themselves that have been long neglected and are sorely in need of healing. Many recall forgotten images of nurturing moments with parents, teachers, and other caregivers.

These new awarenesses can supply men with visions of healthier, more loving relationships, and encourage them to make the most out of their relationships. They can also encourage men to work through their regrets, guilt, shame, and sorrow for the things they could have, should have, or would have done differently in their life.

Inevitably, there are scores of actions or inactions for men to ponder when a loved one has died or they face a significant loss. With hindsight, many men may wish they had done some things differently. They may regret the times when they were stubborn, defensive, or self-righteous. They may regret not saying "I love you" more often, commending others for a job well done, or admitting that they were wrong about something. As they strive for wholeness, some men may reconcile themselves to the realities of what did take place, and accept the past. However difficult to do, they may even forgive themselves for past actions, especially when they see that holding on to their guilt and refusing to forgive themselves has kept them hostage to the past.

The decision to let go of transgressions enables men to loosen their controlling grip on life. They realize that clenching the sands of life too tightly only causes more of it to slip through their fingers.

Transformation hinges on self-acceptance. To be changed by grief a man must allow himself the joy of knowing what he is and what he is not. He must accept himself totally: faults and weaknesses as well as virtues and strengths. He must accept that he makes mistakes and that, at times, he needs support. In his quest for self-acceptance, he must realize that he cannot control the world.

A great deal of freedom comes when a man relinquishes his need to control the world. Life gets simpler, for there are fewer decisions to make, fewer things to plan, fewer standards to live up to. Life becomes something that is lived in the moment, and tomorrow's challenges are left for tomorrow.

Self-acceptance invites calmness. Men feel an inner peace and are more tolerant of the trifling disappointments that fill everyday life. They no longer feel the same pressure to make everything turn out right. The pain of their personal tragedy has not disappeared; rather, it has been absorbed into them. Past and present have fused. Kent Koppelman's story describes such an integration of past and present: his love for Jason has been both cause and cure for his suffering.

Many relational changes occur for men like Kent who strive for wholeness. They develop a new appreciation for others that strengthens their roles as partner, parent, employee, son, sibling, and friend. Many also feel a greater affiliation with other men.

Men who have been transformed by grief often seem less hurried and more introspective. Their demeanor is quiet and filled with pauses; they become more thoughtful, thankful, respectful. Their eyes seem to take in more of the world, and others feel drawn into and included in their gaze.

Differentiations between me and thee, us and them, the self and the other, seem to fall away.

This falling away of differentiations surprises and even intimidates some men. Because they have been conditioned to view the world in terms of status, competition, and strategic alliances, they need time to adjust to the new sense of connectedness they are beginning to feel—a connectedness that extends beyond their relationships with other people to include their relationship with nature and all living matter. Many men grow spiritually, becoming cognizant and appreciative of the beauty of all creation. They have a sense of peace and community unlike anything they have previously felt.

Of course, transformations affect women much as they do men. Life takes on greater clarity for women, and they begin to realize the power they have to recast and redirect their future. Many women see options and opportunities where once they saw only rigid roles and expectations. In the process, they become more trusting of their own intuition and intellect. Some channel their energies into formulating a new vision for their life, while others pursue life-long dreams. Choosing to live more abundantly and intentionally, women become more reflective and passionate about the things that matter most.

In the course of transformation, many men formulate new opinions about their own mortality and about life and death. They become less fearful of death and accept the reality that a lifetime is not forever. They begin to see life as something rare and ephemeral, a valuable currency that they must spend wisely.

As men integrate and transform their loss, they also change their world of meaning. Things once thought to be irrelevant or mundane may now have great significance. For Kent Koppelman, common objects like coins, movie stubs, and a school backpack took on new meaning. These objects became concrete signs of Kent's love for his son, Jason.

The transformational process can usher in a new life for men. Though not what they expected or hoped for, their new life, nevertheless, can be more vital and profound than their old one. Men can experience a new openness about their life and a willingness to let providence guide them. Flooded with new awareness, they can make peace with the past while anticipating the mysteries that still lie ahead.

Cherish the meaning of love

To grieve is to invite change. Inviting change into our lives challenges us to do more than just survive. It calls us to transform our lives so we can become more than we once were. Partners may take dissimilar paths as they transform their lives, but, because of their intimate bond, many will eventually draw closer together. As the drama of change unfolds, women must cherish the meaning of love by remembering what originally brought their partner and them together. Those qualities the woman loved are very likely still there.

We all want to love and be loved in return. To treat a broken heart, we need tenderness, intimacy, and love. Yet the intense pressures of grieving can easily turn a caring relationship into a hostile one. Weak partnerships can be strained almost beyond repair. Though tempting, a woman must not give up on her partner or herself. The threats that grief makes to intimate partnerships must be confronted head-on.

Our different ways of grieving can obscure our vision. To see clearly, women must become empathetic and endeavor to understand how their partner is grieving and why he differs in his style of grieving. Only then will women be able to see past their partner's displays of independence, to discover his true vulnerabilities. Only then will women be able to cherish the meaning of love.

Love creates our dreams and hopes. It sustains us when grief empties our life of meaning. It brings us joy and makes life worth living. Love is the soul of our intimate partnerships. There is common ground in our grief. Join together and live out your love.

About the Contributors

Louis Cerulli has a master's degree in English literature. He lives with his wife in Memphis. He is currently working on a novel and a collection of poetry. Louis volunteers his time at a cancer treatment center where he practices Reiki. He also works as a graphic artist for organizations in the Memphis area.

Jim Amundsen was born in Michigan and has lived in the Midwest all his life. He is an avid movie fan and appreciates science fiction books. In his spare time, Jim enjoys a variety of outdoor activities, especially canoeing and skiing.

J. B. Blair worked for more than forty years as a dentist. He was born in Des Moines, Iowa, and retired to Florida a number of years ago. He volunteers at a free clinic and also takes time for tennis, sailing, and hiking.

Thomas Chalfant and his wife, Patty, have two children. Tom is an active volunteer for a variety of helping organizations and in his free time indulges in his love of fly-fishing and scuba diving. He also dabbles in woodworking.

Richard Friberg is a forensic and clinical psychologist who specializes in applying his skills in the criminal justice system. He is an avid gardener, pianist, traveler, and stamp collector.

John L. Jankord was born in Bloomington, Minnesota, and still resides in the area. He and his wife, Eileen, have a three-year-old daughter, Megan. John enjoys camping, biking, and gardening with his family.

Larry D. Johnson and his wife, Elaine Wynne, are professional storytellers. Larry and Elaine have nine grandchildren and are deciding how just to travel the world, see what's there, and tell stories to grandchildren and anyone else who wants to hear them.

Kent L. Koppelman is from rural Nebraska. He teaches classes on understanding human differences at the University of Wisconsin at La

Crosse. He and his wife have two children, Jason, who was killed in 1989, and Tess, who recently graduated from college. Kent and his wife love to travel and have made several trips abroad.

Jon Masson holds a master's degree in mass communication from Drake University. He is the sports editor of the *La Crosse Tribune*. Previously, he worked as a journalist for the *Phoenix Gazette* and *Colorado Springs Sun*. Jon and his wife, Patrice, and daughter, Gabrielle, live in Onalaska, Wisconsin.

Jim Murrow holds a Ph.D. in marketing and teaches marketing, leadership, strategy, and values analysis at a Midwestern University. His more than twenty years in business have helped him bring reality into the classroom. Jim is a retired black belt and a Vietnam veteran.

Ralph O. Robinson's interests include T'ai Chi, meditation, pottery, fly-fishing, canoeing, and reading. As a scuba divemaster he enjoys filming and editing his underwater videotapes. He and his wife have two living children and reside in Minneapolis with Ranger, their golden retriever. *Follow the Wind: Songs for Stained Souls* is available from The Compassionate Friends.

Robert W. Ross has combined careers as a Protestant minister and full-time academic on the college and university level. He was born in Yuma, Colorado, and continues to do research and writing, though technically retired. Robert has two children and feels that he has led a full life.

About the Author

Elizabeth Levang, Ph.D., is an author, national speaker, and consultant in the fields of human development and psychology. She holds a doctorate in human and organizational systems from the Fielding Institute in Santa Barbara, California. Elizabeth conducts educational programs and lectures on grief and loss, and also consults with corporations and organizations to assist employees who are grieving. Her first book, *Remembering With Love: Messages of Hope for the First Year of Grieving and Beyond*, is also published by Fairview Press.

Elizabeth and her family live in suburban Minneapolis, Minnesota.

Resources

Bereavement

AARP, Widowed Persons Services
601 E St. NW, Washington, DC 20049
202-434-2277; 800-424-3410
Web site: http://www.aarp.org
information and resources; referrals to support groups

Alive Alone, Inc.
11115 Dull Robinson Road, Van Wert, Ohio 45891
education and support for bereaved parents whom death has left childless

American Association of Suicidology
4201 Connecticut Avenue NW, Suite 310, Washington, DC 20008
202-237-2280
Web site: http://www.cyberpsych.org/aas/index.html
E-mail: amyjomc@ix.netcom.com
information and resources; referrals to suicide survivor groups

Bereavement Services, Gundersen Lutheran Medical Center
1910 South Avenue, La Crosse, Wisconsin 54601
608-791-4747; 800-362-9567, ext. 4747
Web site: http://www.gundluth.org/bereave
E-mail: berservs@lhl.gundluth.org
training for healthcare professionals in perinatal bereavement and in comprehensive bereavement programs

The Compassionate Friends, National Office
P.O. Box 3696, Oak Brook, Illinois 60522-3696
630-990-0010
Web site: http://www.jjt.com/ntcf–national/
E-mail: tcf–national@prodigy.com
information and resources for bereaved families who have experienced the death of a child

Families Helping Families, The Jenna Druck Foundation
3636 Fifth Avenue, Suite 201, San Diego, CA 92103
619-294-8000; 619-294-8889
Web site: http://www.jennadruck.org
E-mail: JDFound@aol.com
resources and support for families who have experienced the death of a child

National SHARE Office, St. Joseph's Health Center
300 First Capitol Drive, St. Charles, Missouri 63301-2893
314-947-6164; 800-821-6819
Web site: http://www.NationalSHAREOffice.com
E-mail: SHARE@NationalSHAREOffice.com
resources, support, and referrals for bereaved families

Mothers Against Drunk Driving (MADD)
511 E. John Carpenter Freeway, Suite 700, Irving, Texas 75062-8187
214-744-6233 or 1-800-GET MADD
Web site: http://www.MADD.org
education, resources, and advocacy for bereaved families

Parents of Murdered Children, Inc.
100 E. 8th Street, B-41, Cincinnati, Ohio 45202
513-721-5683; 888-818-POMC
Web site: http://www.pomc.com
E-mail: NatlPOMC@aol.com
information, resources, and support for bereaved families

Pregnancy and Infant Loss Center
1421 East Wayzata Boulevard, Suite 30, Wayzata, Minnesota 55391
952-473-9372
support, resources, and referrals for bereaved families who have experienced
pregnancy or infant loss; resources for bereavement professionals

RESOLVE, INC.
1310 Broadway, Sommerville, Massachusetts 02144-1779
Help line: 617-623-0744
Web site: http://www.resolve.org
E-mail: resolveinc@aol.com
education, advocacy, and support for those experiencing infertility

Health

Alcoholics Anonymous, World Services
P.O. Box 459, New York, NY 10163
212-870-3400
Web site: http://www.alcoholics-anonymous.org/
education, resources, and referrals to support groups

American Cancer Society
24-hour phone: 800-ACS-2345
Web site: http://www.cancer.org
education and referral services; publications and media data on late-breaking research

National AIDS Hotline
800-342-2437
Web site: http://www.ashastd.org
education, referral, and resources for individuals and families

National Cancer Institute
9000 Rockville Pike, Bethesda, Maryland 20892
800-422-6237
Web site: http://www.nci.nih.gov/
information and resources for individuals and families

National Institute of Mental Health
Public Inquiries, Rm 7C02, MSC 8030
5600 Fishers Lane, Rockville, Maryland 20892-8030
301-443-4513
Web site: http://www.nimh.nih.gov
education and publications for families and professionals

Workaholics Anonymous
P.O. Box 289, Menlo Park, California 94026-0289
510-273-9253
Web site: http://www.ai.mit.edu/people/wa

Gamblers Anonymous International Service Office
P.O. 17173 , Los Angeles, California 90017
213-386-8789
Web site: http://www.gamblersanonymous.org
information, resources, and referral to support groups

Sex Addicts Anonymous
P.O. Box 70949, Houston, Texas 77270
713-869-4902
web site: http://www.saa-recovery.org
E-mail: info@saa-recovery.org
information, resources, and referral to support groups

Parenting

National Parent Information Network
University of Illinois, Urbana-Champaign
Children's Research Center, Room 9
51 Gerty Drive, Champaign, Illinois 61820-7469
800-583-4135
Web-site: http://npin.org
resources for parents and those who work with parents

National Center for Fathering
P.O. Box 413888, Kansas City, Missouri 64141
800-593-DADS
Web site: http://www.fathers.com
E-mail: dads@Fathers.com
education, resources, publications, and radio program

National Parenting Center
22801 Ventura Blvd., Woodland Hills, California 91367
800-753-6667
Web site: http://www.tntc.com
advice and information for parents